THE GERMAN SUCCESS CULTURE

The German Success Culture

by Dr. Eike Post
Copyright © 2025
All rights reserved.

First Edition

No part of this book may be reproduced, stored in a retrieval system, or transmitted in any form—whether electronic, mechanical, photocopying, recording, scanning, or otherwise—except for brief quotations in critical reviews or articles, without the prior written permission of the author.

This book is intended solely for educational and informational purposes. The author and publisher are not providing it as legal, financial, or professional advice.

Although best efforts have been made to ensure the accuracy and completeness of this content, the author and publisher make no representations or warranties of any kind and disclaim any implied warranties of fitness for a particular purpose. The information and perspectives presented here may not apply to every individual's unique circumstances.

Neither the author nor the publisher shall be liable for any losses, incidental or consequential damages that may arise, or be alleged to have arisen, directly or indirectly, from the information provided within these pages.

This book offers insights based on the author's experience and the opinions expressed herein are solely those of the author. Readers are encouraged to consult with qualified professionals to tailor advice to their specific needs.

INDEX

1. INTRODUCTION TO GERMAN SUCCESS CULTURE 1

2. SIGNIFICANCE OF CULTURE 9
   - 2.1. What is Culture Anyway? 9
   - 2.2. The Power of Culture 13
   - 2.3. The Idea of a Guiding Culture for Germany 18

3. CREATING A GUIDING CULTURE 26

4. SHARED VISION FOR GERMANY 30

5. THE GERMAN SUCCESS STORY 35

6. CULTURAL DIAGNOSIS OF GERMAN VALUE CULTURE 46

7. SOCIAL RESPONSIBILITY 52
   - 7.1. Respect for Human Dignity 53
   - 7.2. Protecting the Vulnerable 56
   - 7.3. Altruism 57
   - 7.4. Zivilcourage 59
   - 7.5. Welcome Culture 60

8. PLURALISM 66
   - 8.1. Diversity and Tolerance 67
   - 8.2. Sexual Freedom 71
   - 8.3. Religious Freedom 74
   - 8.4. Combating Anti-Semitism 76

9. FEMINISM 79
   - 9.1. Gender Equality 79
   - 9.2. Protection of Women 83
   - 9.3. Respect for Women 85

10. SINCERITY 88
10.1. Honesty 88
10.2. Directness 91
10.3. Tax Compliance 93
10.4. Fairness 95
10.5. Reliability 97

11. PEACEFULNESS 100
11.1. Listening 100
11.2. Consideration 102
11.3. Non-Violence 104
11.4. Pacifism 105

12. DISCIPLINE AND OBEDIENCE 107
12.1. Adherence to Rules 107
12.2. Sense of Duty 111
12.3. Respect for Authority 116
12.4. Cleanliness 119
12.5. Tranquility 123

13. ACCURACY 128
13.1. Punctuality 128
13.2. Perfectionism 131
13.3. Orderliness 133

14. WORK ETHIC 136
14.1. Diligence 136
14.2. Speed 139
14.3. Productivity 140
14.4. Pursuit of Achievement 142

15. KNOWLEDGE SOCIETY 148
15.1. Education 148
15.2. Critical Thinking 151
15.3. Innovation 155

16. LOVE OF NATURE 159
16.1. Connection to Nature 159
16.2. Environmental Awareness...162
16.3. Climate Protection..164
16.4. Animal Love 168

17. SUSTAINABILITY... 171
17.1. Thriftiness..171
17.2. Modesty... 173
17.3. Long-term Thinking.. 175

18. LOYALITÄT 179
18.1. Company Loyalty...179
18.2. Relationship Loyalty 181
18.3. Bindingness.. 183

19. LOVE OF FREEDOM 185
19.1. Bodily Autonomy.. 185
19.2. Personal Space.. 187
19.3. Privacy... 189
19.4. Freedom of Speech 192

20. PERSONAL RESPONSIBILITY 199
20.1. Self-Reliance 199
20.2. Proactivity 202
20.3. Self-Respect 204

21. GOOD MANNERS 208
21.1. Polite Communication 209
21.2. Polite Behavior 212
21.3. Table Manners 214
21.4. Well-Groomed Appearance 217

22. WESTERN ALLIANCES 221
22.1. Solidarity with Israel 221
22.2. Transatlantic Partnership 226
22.3. Champion of Europe 230

23. DEMOCRATIC FOUNDATION 237
23.1. Democracy 237
23.2. Rules of Law 244
23.3. Secularism 249
23.4. Anti-Fascism 251

24. THE GERMAN CULTURE CODE 256

25. GUIDING CULTURE 2.0 271

26. ARGUMENTS AGAINST A GUIDING CULTURE 276

27. NEED FOR A GUIDING CULTURE 282

28. PRESERVATION OF THE GERMAN SUCCESS CULTURE .. 287

1. INTRODUCTION TO GERMAN SUCCESS CULTURE

Imagine you could hold the key to an entire country's success in your hands. What if this success wasn't based on mere luck or chance, but on a unique combination of values and behaviors that have been shaped and refined over generations?

In this book, we embark on an exciting journey into the depths of German success culture. We explore the values and principles that have made Germany an economic and technological powerhouse.

Goal of the Book and Benefits for the Reader

Thank you for deciding to read this book about German success culture. By doing so, you are not only investing your time but also placing your trust in me – and for that, I would like to express my sincere gratitude.

My goal is that you not only gain useful information from this book but also draw inspiration. I have designed the content in such a way that you receive real added value and discover new perspectives.

Specifically, I hope that you will take away the following insights:
- What constitutes the German value culture.
- Why these values are crucial to Germany's success.
- How we can develop a "guiding culture" based on these values that leads to maximum success.
- How such a success culture can support the success of individuals, organizations and even countries.

If you are reading this book as a printed version, I would be happy to send you the ebook, which is fully colored, as a gift. Just send me a picture of you holding your printed version of the book to eikepost@gmail.com.

Should this book offer you added value, I would be very happy if you would rate it on Amazon. Thank you very much!

About Me

For this book, I not only interviewed countless experts worldwide and waded through mountains of literature, but also delved deep into my own treasure chest of experiences. So perhaps you are interested in who is behind these lines.

My name is Eike Post. At just 16 years old, I swapped German school desks for American lecture halls. My studies in business administration, economics, law, and psychology took me to universities in seven different countries. By the age of 26, I had completed three bachelor's degrees, three master's degrees, a law degree, and a doctoral dissertation.

But I didn't just want to accumulate theoretical knowledge, so I founded companies in Shanghai and London while still studying. In the following years, I worked and lived as an entrepreneur and management consultant in the USA, China, Ukraine, Brazil, and many other countries.

1. INTRODUCTION TO GERMAN SUCCESS CULTURE

These journeys through cultures and continents, combined with my theoretical knowledge, have shown me how strongly one's own culture shapes the success of an individual and a country. At the same time, they have opened my eyes to the uniqueness of the German value culture.

Three Reasons for Writing this Book

Three central motives inspired me to write this book:

My personal "value catalog": 25 years ago, when I left Germany, I started to note down the values and behaviors that struck me as typically German. This catalog, enriched by my experiences in over 30 countries, formed the basis for this book.

My expertise in corporate culture: Through my work with corporate cultures, I realized how important a strong culture is for success – both for companies as well as for entire nations.

My concern for Germany's future: I observe how German culture as well as Western culture in general is changing and Germany's success is dwindling because of it.

Value Catalog – The Origin of my Observations

When I left Germany at the age of 16, I became aware of how much my own culture had shaped me. Things that seemed self-evident to me – punctuality, orderliness, respect for rules – suddenly were no longer. This culture shock was the beginning of a journey of self-discovery. I began to note the differences and peculiarities of different cultures and to write down what drives and motivates people in different parts of the world.

Getting to know and integrating into the new culture was always important to me. When I came to a new country, I didn't just want to be a visitor, but to really experience the culture. Whether in the US, Puerto Rico, Brazil, Ukraine, or China – my friends were mostly locals. Unlike many other expats who mainly moved in their own "bubble," I immersed myself deeply in the local culture. In Beijing and Shanghai, for example, my acquaintances from Europe and the USA almost exclusively had contact with other expats, while I was mainly with Chinese people. This is how I became part of society, and yet wherever I went and no matter how much I absorbed the local culture people kept saying: "Oh Eike, you are so German!" My German traits seemed unmistakable.

Over time and through my stays in over 30 countries, this catalog of values and behaviors grew steadily. I realized that people from different cultural backgrounds "tick" differently. With each new country I got to know, my understanding deepened – not only of foreign cultures but above all of my own German culture and how it is different to other cultures.

I realized that growing up in Germany had given me many advantages: a solid basic education, excellent health care, and a good diet. I am grateful to Germany for all these opportunities. But the most valuable gift is German culture itself. This culture, passed down through generations, is a treasure that should be preserved and cherished.

Corporate Culture: My Professional Experience

My professional life has been immersed in the dynamic world of startups and young companies, where I've played the roles of both founder and consultant. This firsthand experience provided invaluable insights into the power of a thoughtfully

1. INTRODUCTION TO GERMAN SUCCESS CULTURE

crafted corporate culture. It's the unseen force that propels a company forward, determining its trajectory and ultimate fate.

Through analyzing and shaping company cultures, I became fascinated by how cultural shifts could dramatically impact a company's success or contribute to its downfall. This led me to ponder a broader question: Could the same principle apply to an entire nation? **Could a country's culture be the key to its flourishing or its decline? And if so could I apply the same principle I used in forming corporate cultures to form a national culture?**

German Culture in Danger: A Wake-Up Call

The third and perhaps most important reason that motivated me to record my findings in this book was the growing concern for the future of German culture. I observed how the culture in Germany was changing rapidly and many of the values that once constituted Germany's strength were losing importance.

At the same time, Germany was losing more and more ground in many areas where it used to be a leader. Countries like the US, China, and various Asian countries overtook Germany – be it in technology, education, or the economy.

The common explanations for Germany's dwindling success – from the Corona crisis to the Ukraine war to the refugee crisis and energy policy – seemed too short-sighted to me. It became increasingly clear to me that the real cause lies deeper: in the change of German culture.

I have seen how unique German culture is and how much it forms the basis for the success of the country. This book is therefore my contribution to preserving and protecting this culture – because without it, Germany loses not only its identity but also its future prospects.

Structure of the Book

The book takes you on a journey through the world of German success culture and is structured as follows:

- **Chapter 2: Definition and Importance of Success Culture and Guiding Culture** Here we look at how a guiding culture can lead a company, but also a country, to success and why it is so important.
- **Chapter 3: Creating a Guiding Culture** We examine how a guiding culture can be defined for companies and how it can increase success. It turns out that the same methodology can also be applied to countries.
- **Chapter 4: The First Element of Guiding Culture – Shared Visions** A clear shared vision is the foundation of a strong culture. This chapter explains why a national vision is crucial for long-term success.
- **Chapter 5: The Second Element of Guiding Culture – The German Success Story** We look at how a positive story about Germany and German history motivates us to build on this success.
- **Chapters 6-23: The Principles of German Value Culture** The main part of the book presents the 17 basic principles of German value culture, which are based on 64 values that have shaped Germany over generations.
- The 17 basic principles are:
    - Social Responsibility
    - Pluralism
    - Feminism

1. INTRODUCTION TO GERMAN SUCCESS CULTURE

- Sincerity
- Peacefulness
- Discipline and Obedience
- Accuracy
- Work Ethic
- Knowledge Society
- Love of Nature
- Sustainability
- Loyalty
- Love of Freedom
- Personal Responsibility
- Good Manners
- Western Alliances
- Democratic Foundation

- **Chapter 24: The Third Element of Guiding Culture – The Cultural Code** Based on the 17 basic principles of German value culture, we define a cultural code as a guideline for daily action.
- **Chapter 25: Guiding Culture 2.0**
  This chapter summarizes the three elements of German guiding culture: guiding vision, success story, and cultural code.
- **Chapter 26: Dangers of a Guiding Culture**
  We highlight the arguments of the critics of a guiding culture.
- **Chapter 27: Need of a Guiding Culture**
  We highlight the arguments of the critics of a guiding culture.

- **Chapter 28: An Outlook on the Future of Guiding Culture**
  This chapter deals with the challenges and opportunities of German guiding culture in the future.

2. SIGNIFICANCE OF CULTURE

This book takes you on an exciting journey of discovery through German culture and its influence on Germany's success story. We want to not only preserve this valuable culture, but also to develop it further and use it as a strong foundation for a successful future.

But before we dive into the fascinating depths of German culture, we should first clarify what we actually mean by "culture." It's a term that often causes confusion, as it holds more than one might initially suspect.

2.1. What is Culture Anyway?

Imagine "culture" as a mysterious garden full of surprises. It not only houses magnificent flowers (the **"Zivilisationskultur"** or "civilization culture"), but also deep-rooted trees that give the garden its structure and stability (the **"Wertekultur"** or "value culture").

Think of "civilization culture" as a treasure chest filled with precious jewels. Imagine majestic buildings like the Cologne Cathedral, the timeless beauty of Goethe's poems, the rousing sounds of Beethoven's music, the cozy get-together at Oktoberfest, or the smell of freshly baked cookies at Christmas time. These are all facets of German civilization culture that inspire and fascinate us.

"Value culture" on the other hand, is the invisible foundation on which society rests. It is the deeply rooted values and principles that guide our thinking and actions - from everyday rules of courtesy to fundamental beliefs like democracy, equality, and respect for nature.

Concept of Culture

civilization culture
- Traditions
- Food
- Customs
- History
- Music
- Literature
- Religion
- Clothing

Value Culture
- Thriftiness
- Obedience
- Discipline
- Order
- Democracy
- Gender Equality
- Work Ethic
- Good manners

The diagram above shows how the concept of culture is divided into two parts: civilizational culture and value culture. Although both are grouped under the term "culture," they express something completely different.

In this book, we talk exclusively about value culture because it is crucial for long-term success – be it of a company, a country, or even personal success. What food or music someone prefers or what literary preferences they have is relatively unimportant in this context. What matters is our behavior and the values on which our behavior is based. It is these values and behaviors that lead to success or failure. That is why we focus on value culture in this book.

Why is civilizational culture less important to us and value culture so crucial? Quite simply: values shape the behavior of a society and directly influence its success. A strong value culture can drive advancement, while weak values accelerate decline.

2. SIGNIFICANCE OF CULTURE

Success Culture

Success is not a coincidence. Sure, some people inherit a fortune, win the lottery, or simply get lucky. But let's be honest: how sustainable is this success really? True, lasting success that endures for generations and achieves great things comes from diligence, perseverance, and the courage to constantly face new challenges.

Remember an athlete who trains for years to win a competition. Or an entrepreneur who builds a successful business with an innovative idea. Behind these successes lies not only talent and luck, but above all hard work, discipline, and the absolute will to succeed. These are all values of a personal or corporate culture that make all the difference.

And the same applies to entire nations! Countries that are economically successful and offer prosperity to their citizens have often achieved this through decades of effort, wise decisions, and a culture that promotes achievement and innovation.

A society that considers laziness and the waste of resources as normal will not be successful in the long run. Likewise, values such as racism or discrimination, which disadvantage people based on gender, origin, or social status, hinder progress and lead to a dead end.

A success culture is like fertile ground that enables maximum success.

Guiding Culture

A guiding culture ("Leitkultur") is a culture created to guide the population to values and behavior that make the organization or the country more successful.

The concept of guiding culture in Germany is often misunderstood as a guide for migrants. But guiding culture is much more than just an integration concept. It is a shared canon of values that provides orientation for all citizens and enables coexistence in our pluralistic society. It defines what is important to us as a society and what goals we are pursuing together.

Imagine a soccer team: to be successful, it needs not only talented individual players but also a common game strategy and clear rules that everyone adheres to. In the same way, a nation needs a guiding culture that aligns all members towards common goals and strengthens cohesion.

The importance of corporate culture has long been recognized in the business world. Successful companies invest a lot of time and energy in building a strong corporate culture that is shared by all employees.

They know that a positive working atmosphere, shared values, and clear goals increase employee motivation and productivity and thus contribute to the company's success.

At the national level, this knowledge is not yet so widespread. But culture is also crucial to the success of a country.

By analyzing and shaping a culture, we can create a guiding culture not only for companies but also for an entire country. The goal of this guiding culture is to become more successful. Therefore, guiding culture and success culture are almost identical. Success culture is the culture that leads to maximum success. Guiding culture is the attempt to influence the values and behavior of each member in such a way that it leads to success.

2.2. The Power of Culture

Culture is crucial for companies! Every manager and HR employee understands that a company's culture is the basis for success.

But while this connection has not yet been comprehensively researched at the national level, it is already part of the general know-how of management consultants in the corporate context.

The Power of Corporate Culture: The Key to Success

Just type "culture and success" into your search engine. You'll be flooded with articles about corporate culture! The business world seems to have long since uncovered the secret: a strong corporate culture is the key to success. But why is hardly anyone talking about the importance of culture for the success of an entire country? This connection is just as important!

Let's first take a look at the corporate world and then see how these findings can be applied to entire nations.

My years of experience as an entrepreneur and consultant have shown me how a strong corporate culture can make the difference between mediocrity and true success. At first, I was in the dark. I stumbled through the entrepreneurial world without a clue what corporate culture even was, let alone how to shape it in a targeted way.

Corporate Culture is Not a Buzzword, but a Game Changer

The turning point came through a conversation with an experienced mentor. His questions about our corporate culture hit me like a punch in the face. I suddenly realized that I had no answers. Until then, I had simply taken the culture of my company for granted.

My mentor opened my eyes: corporate culture is not an abstract concept, but a central factor for long-term success. It is the invisible bond that holds a team together, the common language that creates understanding, and the compass that sets the direction.

From Theory to Practice

I plunged into the topic, read books, watched videos, talked to experts. But knowledge alone is not enough. So I involved my team and together we defined our vision and values, openly discussed our cooperation and expectations.

The result was our own culture code - not a dusty set of rules, but a living document with concrete behaviors for everyday life.

And it worked! Motivation increased, a sense of responsibility grew, cooperation flourished. Our company had a new drive, and success was not long in coming.

Can Culture Drive an Entire Country Forward?

While the influence of culture on the success of companies is undisputed, the connection between culture and the success of an entire country is often overlooked. We think of national success in terms of resources, education, peace... But what if culture is the decisive factor that makes the difference? What if the values and beliefs of a society form the breeding ground for economic prosperity and social progress?

Max Weber and the Protestant Ethic

More than 120 years ago, the German sociologist Max Weber asked this question: Is there a connection between the culture of a country and its economic success? In his influential work "The Protestant Ethic and the Spirit of Capitalism," he examined this connection and came to a fascinating realization.

Weber argued that certain religious beliefs of Protestantism, particularly Calvinism, produced a specific value culture that fueled the rise of modern capitalism in Northern Europe and the USA. This "Protestant success formula" was based on several core values:

- **Asceticism and hard work:** Protestant teachings emphasized a disciplined and abstemious lifestyle. Pleasure and luxury were rejected, while hard work and thrift were considered signs of divine grace. This attitude created a strong work ethic and a tireless pursuit of economic success.
- **Vocation and profession:** Work was not seen merely as a means to an end, but as a divine calling to be fulfilled with a sense of duty and dedication. This inner drive led to a high degree of commitment and willingness to perform.
- **Capital accumulation:** Instead of spending wealth on personal luxury, reinvestment in one's own business was considered virtuous. This practice led to an accumulation of capital that could be used for further growth and innovation.

- **Rationalization:** Protestantism promoted a rational and methodical approach to everyday life, which also carried over into the economy. Systematic planning, efficiency, and a calculating approach became important principles of economic action.

Max Weber's analysis shows that cultural values are more than just beliefs - they have the power to shape economic systems and influence the prosperity of an entire country. He established a clear link between the Protestant value culture and the rise of capitalism, which led to unprecedented economic success.

Successful Value Culture Leads to Economic Success

Weber's theory can be simplified as follows:

Religion → Value Culture → Capitalism → Success

In our analysis, we focus on the direct link between value culture and success, regardless of the specific religion or economic system. We assume that a culture that promotes certain positive values favors a country's economic success, which we represent as follows:

Value Culture → Success

Post-war divided Germany offers a fascinating example of how "Wertekultur" (value culture) significantly influences a country's success, regardless of its economic system. While West Germany's economy developed more rapidly under capitalism, East Germany was also comparatively successful within the socialist bloc. This suggests that the shared cultural foundation, which included values such as discipline and a strong work ethic, had a decisive impact on economic success, independent of the prevailing economic system.

The Rediscovery of Culture

Although Max Weber's groundbreaking analysis was published over a century ago, the link between "Wertekultur" and success was long forgotten. Both sociologists and economists have surprisingly neglected this connection, and culture and economy have been viewed in isolation in the past.

Fortunately, more and more economists today recognize the importance of culture for success - not only for companies, but also for entire nations. Numerous recent studies confirm an impressive correlation between culture and economic success. Countries with a culture that promotes values such as trust, innovation, and long-term thinking generally perform much better economically.

Germany as an Example of Success

The answer becomes clear when you look at the research findings of Max Weber and more recent economists: There is a clear connection between culture and economic success. Let's take a closer look at this connection.

Germany has a long history of success - whether as an export champion, a global innovation center, or through its world-leading companies in various industries. But what made this success possible? How could a country that was once fragmented and backward rise to become one of the most powerful economic nations in the world?

Was it the wealth of natural resources? Definitely not. Germany has relatively few natural resources compared to other countries. So what is the explanation? The answer lies in the "Wertekultur." The unique blend of diligence, discipline, punctuality, thrift, education, and a strong sense of duty has transformed Germany into an economic powerhouse. These qualities created fertile ground for innovation, economic progress, and social cohesion.

Both Weber's analysis and current research findings, as well as Germany's success, impressively demonstrate that cultural values have enormous power. They shape the thinking and actions of a society, influence its economic decisions, and ultimately determine its success in all areas.

So if culture is so crucial to a country's success, shouldn't we actively work to align our culture in a way that enables maximum success - just as companies do?

2.3. The Idea of a Guiding Culture for Germany

The idea of defining and promoting a German culture is far from new. Back in the 1990s, the German-Syrian intellectual Bassam Tibi coined the term "Leitkultur" (guiding culture). Tibi, a bridge-builder between cultures, wanted to create a common foundation of values in an increasingly multicultural society.

Leitkultur - More Than Just Integration

Tibi's approach initially focused primarily on immigrants. He wanted to provide them with a "Leitkultur"(guiding culture) as a compass to help them find their way in German society. However, Tibi's vision did not extend to thoroughly examining

German culture itself and considering how it could make Germany as a whole more successful.

Of course, a guiding culture is important for integration. It can help immigrants find their place in German society and actively participate in social life. But its potential is much greater! A clearly defined guiding culture would benefit all Germans, not just those with a migration background. It could form a strong foundation that would make us even more successful as a society.

Therefore, a guiding culture should not only aim for integration, but also promote Germany as a whole - in all areas. It's not just about people with a migration background, but about every one of us.

Before we develop a modern guiding culture with a culture code, let's take a look at the existing ideas in this debate. What has already been proposed? What are the strengths and weaknesses of these approaches?

Bassam Tibi's Guiding Culture: A Solid Foundation, But Too Abstract

Bassam Tibi defined five central pillars for the German guiding culture, which were to serve as the basis for the integration of migrants:

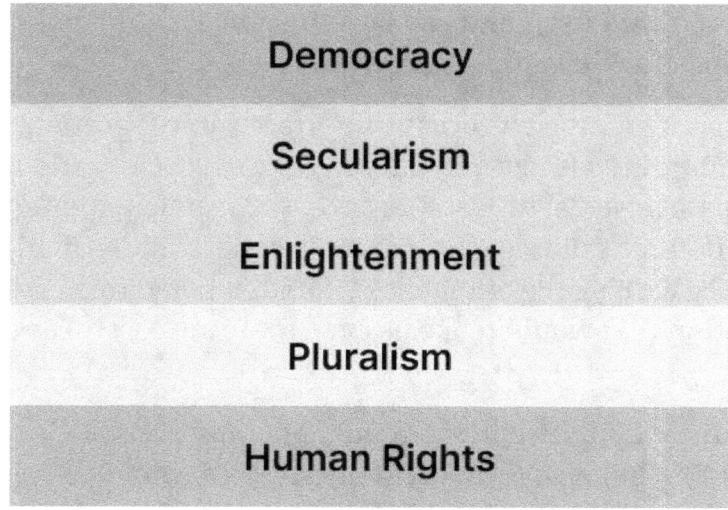

- **Democracy:** The participation of citizens as a cornerstone of a vibrant and functioning democracy.
- **Secularism:** The separation of church and state to ensure freedom of religion and create a neutral public space.
- **Enlightenment:** Science, reason, and education as engines for progress and individual development.
- **Pluralism:** Diversity in cultural, religious, and ethnic terms as an enrichment for society.
- **Human Rights:** The inalienable rights of every individual as the foundation of a just and free society.

These basic principles are undoubtedly of great importance, and as we will see, they are all part of our definition of German guiding culture.

However, Tibi's model is somewhat rudimentary; it lacks the necessary concreteness. The five pillars represent a solid philosophical foundation, but they do not provide detailed guidance for everyday life. A guiding culture should not only convey abstract principles but also formulate tangible and understandable instructions for daily life.

It is not enough to tell migrants: "Integrate and observe these five principles – value human rights, support democracy, separate religion from the state, strive for education, and be tolerant." These demands are too vague and difficult to implement if they are not linked to concrete recommendations for action.

A guiding culture must therefore offer more: it should contain clear, practical instructions for action that help people to live and implement these principles in everyday life.

The 10 Commandments of Guiding Culture: More Concrete, But Incomplete

In 2017, Interior Minister Thomas de Maizière presented a ten-point plan that was intended to define the essence of "German guiding culture." This plan, often referred to as the "10 Commandments of Guiding Culture," was intended to serve as a guide for harmonious coexistence and successful integration.

What points did this ten-point plan contain?

1. **Education for all**: Everyone should be willing to continuously develop and learn throughout their lives.
2. **Stronger together**: Everyone bears responsibility and should actively contribute to society.
3. **Acknowledge the past**: German history, with all its ups and downs, must be accepted and reflected upon.
4. **Appreciate culture**: Respect for the achievements of German culture and its cultivation should be a matter of course.

5. **Respect faith**: Churches, mosques, and synagogues are connecting elements of society.
6. **Diversity**: Tolerance towards different lifestyles is essential.
7. **Patriotism without hate**: One should be able to love one's country without devaluing other nations.
8. **Accept Western ties**: Germany's cultural and political anchoring in the West should be recognized.
9. **Share common memories**: Cultivating collective memories, such as sporting successes and regional traditions, promotes cohesion.
10. **Ban the burqa**: A sign of transparency and openness by rejecting the full veil.

De Maizière's "10 Commandments of Guiding Culture" met with mixed reactions. On the one hand, there was praise for the clear guidelines, but on the other hand, there was sharp criticism, especially regarding the burqa ban, which some saw as an encroachment on personal and religious freedoms.

One advantage of these ten commandments is their tangible concreteness compared to the rather abstract principles of Bassam Tibi. They provide clear rules of conduct.

However, the German value culture is much more complex and extends far beyond these ten points. A truly comprehensive guiding culture must be broader in order to capture the diversity of German culture and values in all its facets.

Some of these rules of conduct overshoot the mark. For example, rule 3: "Acknowledge the past," rule 4: "Appreciate culture," and rule 9: "Share common memories." These rules, which are based on recognition, appreciation, and memories, concern individual preferences and have little relevance for the success of a successful society.

Everyday Culture According to Bernhard Schlink: The Focus on Concrete Behavior

Right after de Maizière had presented his "10 Commandments" Bernhard Schlink, a German lawyer, author, and philosopher, joined the debate. In the Frankfurter Allgemeine Zeitung, an important newspaper in Germany, he presented his idea of "everyday culture as guiding culture" ("Alltagskultur als Leitkultur").

Schlink believes that a guiding culture (*Leitkultur*) should not be based on abstract principles, as in Bassam Tibi's model. Instead, he advocates for a guiding culture rooted in everyday behaviors—things we all know and understand, whether we've lived in Germany all our lives or have recently arrived.

For Schlink, it's not about civilization culture—such as food, music, or religion. In a liberal society, everyone should be free to practice their own civilization culture. What he focuses on is value culture: the shared values and behaviors that shape our communal life.

Schlink identifies a set of values that should serve as guidelines for migrants in Germany:
- Good manners and consideration
- Mutual respect
- Willingness to help others
- A sense of responsibility and achievement
- Respect for German traditions
- Honesty and reliability

- Non-violence

Schlink emphasizes that these everyday behavioral rules are crucial for harmonious coexistence. They form the foundation for a respectful togetherness and significantly contribute to avoiding conflicts and strengthening the social fabric.

However, Schlink's values alone are not enough to fully capture the deep complexity of German culture and its diverse patterns of behavior. In fact, these everyday rules are less a specific guide to living in Germany and more universal principles that make every person a good citizen.

Absolute Confusion, Even Among Supporters of Guiding Culture

Although the guiding culture debate has been raging for decades, and despite the guiding culture proposals discussed above, there is still a Babylonian confusion of tongues: what exactly is guiding culture anyway? Even in the self-proclaimed "guiding culture party" CDU, no one seems to really know.

If you ask CDU members at party conferences what guiding culture means to them, you get answers that range between curious and bizarre:

- "Guiding culture is a framework for action... We have a beautiful landscape. We have a food culture, we have a drinking culture."
- "The Cannstatter Wasen (a folk festival) is part of guiding culture for me."
- "A good coexistence includes something good to drink, which is why wine is part of German guiding culture."

- Matthias Middelberg, Member of the Bundestag: "Milk is also part of guiding culture; because I like to drink it. But guiding culture can also differ regionally."
- Philipp Amthor, Member of the Bundestag: "It's not about dictating whether I shake someone's hand. It's about a broad discussion."

Admittedly, you have to smile. But behind the humor lurks a serious problem: the absolute cluelessness about what guiding culture is actually supposed to be. Are wine, milk, and folk festivals really the cornerstones of our identity? Does that mean that if you don't drink wine or avoid folk festivals, you are less German? If that is the definition of guiding culture, then cheers and bon appétit!

These statements show: Many, especially politicians, call for a guiding culture without even knowing what they mean by it. They act as if guiding culture is something self-evident that you simply feel. But without a clear definition, the term remains nebulous and helps neither with integration nor with strengthening our culture. On the contrary: if guiding culture is defined so superficially, it tends to exclude rather than unite.

So how could a clear and contemporary guiding culture be defined? We will examine this in more detail in the next chapter.

3. CREATING A GUIDING CULTURE

Companies have long recognized that a strong corporate culture is the key to success. They invest time and energy to promote loyalty, motivation, and top performance. But what about the culture of an entire country? Can it be shaped in the same targeted way to boost national success? We believe it can.

Unfortunately, at the country level, culture is often seen as an unchangeable constant, as if it were set in stone. It is assumed that one is not able to consciously shape or change a culture.

While there have been, as we have seen above, efforts in Germany to define a guiding culture, these have so far been only rudimentary and have mainly served to provide guidance only to migrants. A real attempt to align German culture with the success of the country, as companies do with their corporate culture, is still lacking.

The potential of a strong national culture is enormous. It can not only strengthen the sense of togetherness and promote integration, but also serve as a driver for economic success, social justice, and sustainable development.

Creating a National Guiding Culture: But How?

It is time to stop taking culture for granted and start actively shaping it and aligning it with the future. And this is precisely the goal of this book: to diagnose the German value culture and align it in such a way that it leads to maximum success, in other words to create a success culture. Since something like this has not yet been done at the country level, the question arises: How do we do this?

3. CREATING A GUIDING CULTURE

There is hope for us, because many successful companies have already developed proven methods for shaping their corporate culture. These methods can serve as inspiration for us to shape a strong guiding culture at the national level as well.

Five Steps to a Successful Corporate Culture

Even though there is no universal method for creating a guiding culture for a company, a specific five-step process has proven to be particularly successful:

1. **Define a vision:** A strong corporate culture begins with a clear, inspiring vision that goes beyond mere business goals and gives employees meaning and motivation.
2. **Develop the success story:** Every company has a unique story to tell. This story creates an emotional foundation and strengthens the sense of community.
3. **Diagnose the current culture:** Before changes can be made, the existing culture must be thoroughly analyzed to identify strengths and weaknesses.
4. **Establish a cultural code:** Core values and concrete behavioral norms form culture code, which is the heart of corporate culture. They provide orientation and create a common understanding.
5. **Anchor the guiding culture:** The cultural code must be made visible and tangible in everyday life.

As we will see, this five-step process can be used not only for corporate culture but also for creating a guiding culture for Germany.

Diversity and Shared Values: The Key to Success

An important aspect of a successful corporate culture is the combination of diversity and shared values. Modern companies actively promote the diversity of their employees - people of different religions, cultures, countries, and with different life stories are very welcome.

Why this focus on diversity? Because companies have realized that different perspectives and experiences increase creativity and innovation. A diverse team can look at problems from different angles and thus often find unconventional and more effective solutions.

At the same time, successful companies ensure that all employees share a common compass of values and adhere to certain rules of conduct. These shared values form the foundation for a strong corporate culture and create a sense of belonging. They serve as a guide in everyday working life and promote cooperation.

It is precisely this combination of diversity and shared values that we should also strive for when defining a guiding culture at the national level. It is about leaving room for individual cultural expression while creating a strong sense of cohesion through shared values and behaviors. A guiding culture that sees diversity as an enrichment and at the same time offers a common foundation of values on which we can build a strong and sustainable society.

3. CREATING A GUIDING CULTURE

Shaping the German Guiding Culture

Based on these findings, we can apply the same process that companies use to create a guiding culture for Germany, with these 5 steps:

1. Define vision
2. Work out a success story
3. Diagnosing current culture
4. Set culture code
5. Anchor the guiding culture

Through this five-step process, we create a German guiding culture that rests on three pillars:

1. **A shared guiding vision:** An inspiring vision that gives us orientation as a nation and leads us on a common path into the future.
2. **A success story:** A true story about the German past that inspires and motivates us to build on what our ancestors have built.
3. **A cultural code:** A code with clear values and rules of conduct that shape daily interaction.

In the following, we will first deal with the shared guiding vision for Germany, then define an inspiring German success story, and finally, in the main part of the book, address the cultural code with over 60 guiding values and the derived rules of conduct.

4. SHARED VISION FOR GERMANY

A shared vision is like a compass for Germany, that shows the country where it wants to steer as a nation.

Just as a successful corporate culture depends on every employee knowing the company's goals, a country and its citizens also need a clear idea of its objectives. Only when we know where we want to go can we shape the path together.

Therefore, the first step in creating a guiding culture is always to define shared visions:

1. Define vision
2. Work out a success story
3. Diagnosing current culture
4. Set culture code
5. Anchor the guiding culture

From Personal Goals to National Ambitions

Most people have clear personal goals: They know what they want to achieve for themselves, their families, or their careers. But what about goals for the country we live in? Here, too, it is possible and even necessary to have shared national goals. If all of us work towards a common vision for our country, this can significantly increase our countries performance.

Historical Examples of Strong National Visions

Between 1933 and 1945, the National Socialists succeeded in mobilizing the population with clear, common goals. Even though these goals were reprehensible and caused great suffering, it is undeniable that Germany achieved enormous economic and military success during this period.

After the war, we saw another example: the reconstruction of Germany after its total destruction. The shared vision of reconstruction led to an incredible effort that quickly made Germany one of the world's leading economic nations again.

Another impressive example is Singapore: Once a small, underdeveloped country, Singapore set clear goals and motivated its citizens to become one of the world's most successful economies through education, hard work, and the fight against corruption. In just a few decades, Singapore went from being one of the poorest countries in the world to a global success story, with a current average income that is almost twice as high as in Germany.

These examples show: A clear national vision can unleash enormous power and lead to extraordinary success.

It is crucial that we, as a nation, work towards the same goals, instead of each pursuing their own ideas of what Germany should become. Visions should be goals shared by the majority of Germans and that move our country forward.

Six Goals for a Strong Germany

Looking back at what has made Germany successful in the past, and considering what most Germans want for the future of their country, we can define six guiding visions for Germany:
- Successful
- Peaceful
- Beautiful

- Just & Equitable
- Sustainable
- Inclusive

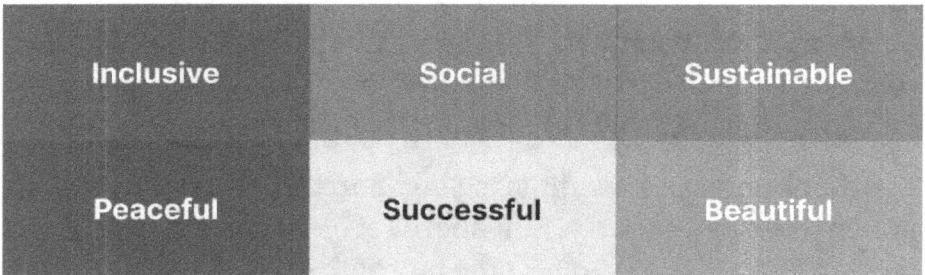

These six goals can unite and motivate us as a nation to work together towards a better future for Germany.

A Successful Germany

A successful Germany is a country that is a global leader and sets standards in many areas – be it in business, science, education, or technology. Success here means not only material prosperity but also innovative strength, stability, and international recognition.

A Peaceful Germany

A peaceful Germany is more than just the absence of war. It is a country that radiates stability both internally and externally. A place where conflicts are resolved not through violence, but through dialogue and diplomatic measures. Peace means social harmony, low crime rates, and an active role in international peacebuilding.

4. SHARED VISION FOR GERMANY

A Beautiful Germany

A beautiful Germany is a country that appreciates and cares for its natural and built environment. It is the preservation of our majestic forests, picturesque coastlines, and sparkling lakes. It is the cleanliness of our streets and squares and the preservation of our historical architecture and monuments.

A Just & Equitable Germany

A just and equitable Germany is more than just a well-developed social system. It is a country where we stand up for each other and take responsibility for each other. A place where everyone, regardless of origin, income, or social status, has access to the basic necessities of life: education, healthcare, and social security.

A Sustainable Germany

Sustainability is more than just a trend – it is a way of life that aims to use our resources responsibly to meet the needs of the present without compromising the future. A sustainable Germany actively takes responsibility for environmental protection, biodiversity, and reducing the negative impacts of human actions.

An Inclusive Germany

Inclusion goes far beyond tolerance – it means actively shaping a society where everyone, regardless of origin, gender, religion, or sexual orientation, not only has equal rights but truly feels a sense of belonging and appreciation. An inclusive Germany sees diversity as a strength and enrichment.

These six visions – success, peace, beauty, social responsibility, sustainability, and inclusion – form a compass that shows the way. They are a shared vision for Germany that inspires and motivates Germans to actively shape the future.

A Vision Needs a Success Story

A shared vision is the first step in building a unifying culture. Yet, visions alone are not enough. For true progress, it's essential to understand the roots of our strengths and challenges. Germany's history—its achievements as well as its mistakes—offers lessons that can help shape a stronger, more inclusive future.

Now that a vision is defined, it's time to look back and transform history into a success story that can inspire and guide a path forward, both within Germany and as a model for others. Through resilience, reflection, and shared goals, we can create a narrative that encourages unity, not only within Germany but also as a broader example of positive change.

5. THE GERMAN SUCCESS STORY

A success story is a narrative about the origins, struggles, and triumphs of a company, organization, or country. Such a success story is crucial for members of that organization or country to realize they are part of something special.

Therefore, the second step in creating a guiding culture is to highlight the success story:

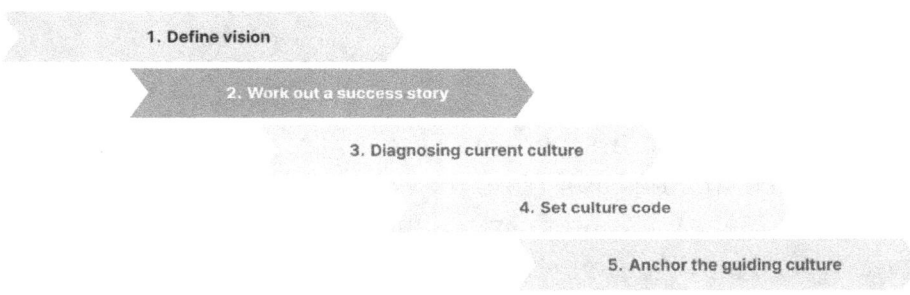

Importance of a Company Story

Before we examine why a success story is important for countries, let's first look at the success stories of companies, as it is common practice for companies to define positive narratives.

For the development of a successful corporate culture, a company story creates an emotional connection between the organization and its stakeholders – be it customers, investors, or especially its own employees. It serves not only as the basis for the company's values and visions but also as a guide for daily action and long-term development.

Here are some examples of companies that masterfully use their stories:

Company Story of The Body Shop

"In a cosmetics industry that uses many toxic ingredients and conducts cruel animal testing, The Body Shop was committed to fighting these practices from the very beginning. Their goal was to offer natural, non-toxic products without animal testing, protecting both animals and consumers."

This company story motivates people to be part of a movement for a sustainable and ethical future.

Company Story of Apple

"Originally, computers were only accessible to wealthy people and large companies. But from the very beginning, Apple wanted to make computers affordable and easy to use for everyone. Despite unfair competition and numerous attempts to copy their innovations, Apple remained true to its vision: innovation and a superior user experience for everyone."

Apple's story isn't just about computers; it's about empowerment. It's the narrative of technology democratized, of sleek design made accessible to everyone. This resonates deeply, fueling the aspirations of millions who dream of working at Apple and captivating hundreds of millions more who choose Apple products as extensions of their own identity.

Company Story of Black Lives Matter (BLM)

"The BLM movement is dedicated to fighting police brutality and promoting equality. Its history is rooted in centuries of oppression and enslavement of black people by white colonial powers. The movement reminds us that many generations before us fought for equality and sacrificed their lives for it."

This organizational story motivates activists to continue the fight for more justice and equality.

All these examples demonstrate the power of a strong company story in creating a loyal and passionate workforce, customers, and members.

A compelling company story explains why the company was founded, what problems it wanted to solve, and what obstacles had to be overcome along the way. It tells of the passion and visions of the founders and the values that drive the company to this day.

An inspiring story conveys to employees that they are part of a mission that began long before them. This awareness strengthens the feeling of carrying on the efforts and legacy of their predecessors. Every employee feels like a guardian of this mission and is willing to do their part to contribute to its success.

Countries and Their National Stories

Not only companies but also entire nations use the power of inspiring stories to instill pride and belonging in their citizens. Such national narratives motivate the population to preserve their cultural heritage and act with pride. Two outstanding examples of this are France and the USA.

Success Story of France

"A country that has enriched the world with its culture and science and played a dominant role in history. Despite internal inequality, France achieved the path to equality through the French Revolution, which took place under the slogan 'Liberté,

Egalité, Fraternité'. This revolution not only shaped modern France but also promised democracy and freedom for peoples around the world."

This success story of France is deeply ingrained in the French psyche, propels them forward, inspiring them to build upon the triumphs of their ancestors and contribute to a legacy that has shaped the world.

Success Story of the USA

"Founded on the desire for freedom, America became a country that attracted people from all over the world in search of liberty. The American Revolution led to the Constitution, which enshrined inalienable rights for all Americans. Time and again, the USA had to fight in wars for freedom and democracy, not only for itself but also for the rest of the world. This USA is widely regarded as the leader of a free and democratic world."

The American story is a narrative that evokes fierce pride in every American, a pride so potent that any perceived challenge to it — like athletes taking a knee during the national anthem — sparks intense debate.

This highlights the profound impact of a national story; it shapes not just identity, but also the very boundaries of acceptable dissent.

This positive narrative is being challenged by activists pushing for a new narrative, called the 1619 project. This narrative shifts the focus from 1776 and the ideals of liberty to 1619 and the harsh realities of slavery. This alternative narrative, though not intended to erase the past, has the potential to disrupt deeply held beliefs about American identity and the foundations upon which the nation was built.

5. THE GERMAN SUCCESS STORY

Because of this, the *1619 Project* poses a fundamental challenge to the traditional American narrative, one that influences not just historical understanding but also collective identity, pride, and cultural aspirations. By reframing the founding of America around 1619, when the first enslaved Africans were brought to Virginia, it shifts focus from the ideals symbolized by 1776 to the systemic injustices of slavery, which it argues are foundational to American development. This alternate narrative invites Americans to confront uncomfortable truths about inequality and racism as integral to the country's formation.

While I'm not an expert in American history and cannot definitively speak to which account holds more historical accuracy, I recognize the impact of each narrative on American identity and collective ambition. The traditional narrative, centered on the ideals of freedom, self-determination, and equal opportunity, fuels a sense of pride that many view as essential to a positive national identity and the success-oriented culture the U.S. is known for. Conversely, the revised narrative risks fostering a sense of collective guilt and shame, which, while prompting critical reflection, may also undermine confidence in America's core values and lead to cynicism rather than optimism. In this way, the first narrative supports a pathway to national pride and drive, while the second could be perceived as discouraging, potentially impacting the broader "success culture" that has historically motivated American progress.

Negative German History

Very few Germans have a positive connection to German history. Rather, there is a shame in being German.

This is also due to the fact that in school Germans hear something like the following story about the essence of Germany:

"We Germans have written some of the darkest chapters in human history. Especially during National Socialism in the 1930s and 40s, our ancestors promoted the systematic extermination of millions of people, particularly the Jewish population. Six million Jews were murdered in the Holocaust, along with millions of others who were considered 'unworthy of life.'"

Our ancestors also showed their cruelty during the colonial era. In what is now Namibia, they committed genocide against the Herero and Nama. Tens of thousands were murdered, driven into the desert, or imprisoned in concentration camps, where they died of hunger and disease.

And not to forget are the two world wars, in which Germans killed countless civilians and waged brutal warfare, such as the scorched earth war in the Soviet Union, where they burned down conquered villages."

This is the story that many Germans have internalized. However, such notions do not inspire people to take up the legacy of their ancestors and continue what they built.

And while the above story is factually correct, it ignores 99% of German history. Germans can be proud of this 99%, and it should inspire them to continue the positive legacy. So it's not about telling a sugarcoated version of German history where Germany has always acted for the good of humanity – that would be a lie. Rather, it's about not just looking at the negative aspects but also appreciating the many positive achievements.

The German Success Story

While it is important to acknowledge the dark sides of the past, we should not forget to look at the light when considering the German founding story. Because Germany has undoubtedly written an impressive success story that has shaped the world in almost every area: intellectually, economically, socially, and ecologically.

Intellectual Rise: Germany as the Cradle of Philosophy

In the 16th century, Germany was still a patchwork of small principalities, far removed from the great powers of the time, such as India, China, or the Ottoman Empire. But while the country lagged behind economically, its thinkers' minds were buzzing.

In the 18th century, during the Enlightenment, German philosophy literally exploded, producing giants like Immanuel Kant, whose "Critique of Pure Reason" shook the foundations of modern philosophy. Schiller and Herder, other luminaries of this era, shaped idealism and humanism. These thinkers not only formed the intellectual backbone of Europe but also laid the foundation for a culture of critical thinking that still distinguishes Germany today. No other country has produced such an abundance of revolutionary ideas that still influence the world.

Economic Rise: Germany as a Global Economic Power

Germany rose not only intellectually but also economically. After the Napoleonic Wars, an unprecedented rise began. By 1870, Germany had already overtaken France in per capita income, and victory in the Franco-Prussian War in 1871 cemented its position as a rising power. But that was just the beginning. In 1890, Germany even surpassed Great Britain and became the second largest economy in the world, second only to the USA.

Even the total collapse after the Second World War could not break the German entrepreneurial spirit. With the legendary "Wirtschaftswunder" (economic miracle), Germany proved its incredible resilience and will to rebuild. The GDR, as the economically strongest country in the Eastern Bloc, underscored this impressive achievement.

In the 1960s, Germany became the world export champion, and in 1973 it again achieved the second highest gross domestic product per capita worldwide. A triumph of diligence, innovation, and the unwavering belief in a better future.

Social Revolutions: Germany as a Pioneer of Justice

Germany was not only economically successful but also socially progressive. As early as 1848, Marx and Engels laid the foundation for a worldwide movement to improve the living conditions of the working class with the "Communist Manifesto."

Bismarck's social laws set global standards for social security, and Germany was one of the first countries to grant women the right to vote. Germany showed the world that technological and economic success can go hand in hand with social progress.

5. THE GERMAN SUCCESS STORY

Technological Innovations: Germany's Inventive Spirit Revolutionizes the World

Germany has always been a land of pioneers and visionaries. In 1886, Karl Benz set the world in motion when he invented the first practical automobile. A few years later, Wilhelm Conrad Röntgen revolutionized medicine with the discovery of X-rays. In 1905, Albert Einstein fundamentally changed our understanding of the universe with the theory of relativity. Quantum mechanics and nuclear fission are further examples of German inventions that have shaped the world. Germany was and is a country that shapes the future.

Sustainability - Germany as the pioneer

Germany recognized the importance of environmental protection early on and founded the world's first Ministry of the Environment in 1971. The green movement, which began in Germany, has spread globally, and with the energy transition, Germany once again set standards for ecological sustainability.

Germany's history is an inspiring success story that shows that the country has been and can be again a leader in almost all areas. It is a testament to the indomitable German spirit, which is always capable of peak performance. If Germany remembers its culture of success, it has a bright future ahead of it.

Short Version of Germany's Success Story

A short version of this success story of Germany would look something like this:

Germany, a nation that has constantly reinvented itself. From the cradle of the Enlightenment, where thinkers shaped the world with their revolutionary ideas, to groundbreaking inventions like the automobile and X-rays – Germany has been a land of innovation and progress.

From a fragmented country, a global economic power emerged. But the country was also a pioneer in social justice and set standards for sustainability.

Germany is not only a land of inventors and thinkers, but also a land committed to a better world.

This is the positive narrative about Germany and the German ancestors.

The negative narrative dwells on the somber aspects of its history, highlighting periods of turmoil and conflict, while the other celebrates a legacy rich in innovation, resilience, and social progress. Both narratives hold truths that reflect different facets of German history, but it is the positive narrative that ignites inspiration and motivation among the German population.

By embracing this uplifting perspective, Germans can take pride in their accomplishments and responsibilities, using their historical successes as a springboard for addressing contemporary challenges.

Just as the American experience demonstrates the power of narrative in shaping national character, so too can Germany harness its positive legacy to create a future marked by innovation and inclusivity.

While a clear guiding vision and Germany's success story help us define the national goals and inspire Germans, the next necessary step is to carefully analyze the present. Only through an honest diagnosis of the cultural strengths and weaknesses

5. THE GERMAN SUCCESS STORY

can one recognize which cultural elements are driving Germany forward and which may be holding it back.

6. CULTURAL DIAGNOSIS OF GERMAN VALUE CULTURE

Previously, we outlined five steps to define a culture:
1. Define the vision
2. Develop the success story
3. Diagnose the current culture
4. Establish a culture code
5. Anchor the guiding culture

Having already agreed on a shared guiding vision and a compelling success story, the next crucial step is upon us: an assessment of the German value culture.

1. Define vision
2. Work out a success story
3. Diagnosing current culture
4. Set culture code
5. Anchor the guiding culture

Cultural Diagnosis: From Company to Country

In the corporate world, cultural diagnoses are established tools for uncovering an organization's strengths and weaknesses. Employee surveys, data analysis, and behavioral observations provide valuable insights into the corporate culture. But how can this approach be applied to an entire country?

6. CULTURAL DIAGNOSIS OF GERMAN VALUE CULTURE

We can utilize similar methods here as well:

1. **Surveys:** We survey people in Germany, Germans abroad, and foreigners living in Germany. These diverse perspectives provide valuable insights into German culture.
2. **Data analysis:** External data, such as crime statistics, data on marriage duration, or studies on working conditions, help us identify cultural trends and social developments.
3. **Behavioral observation:** We observe how Germans interact in different areas of life – professional, private, or public. Particularly interesting are the differences in behavior compared to other nations: How do they treat each other? How do they react to conflict?

My Personal Quest for the Essence of Germans

When I had the idea of defining a guiding culture for Germany, I knew it wouldn't be an easy task. Fortunately, I had been unconsciously preparing for this step for years. As early as 16 years old, during my first stays abroad, I began to attentively observe and record the differences compared to Germany.

For over 20 years now, I have lived mostly abroad, residing in more than 20 countries. Each new country brought valuable insights into my own culture. But almost every year, I returned to Germany for a few months. This constant switching between cultures offered me a unique opportunity to view Germany from an outside perspective, gaining deeper insights.

From afar, I noticed behaviors that seemed self-evident to me in Germany, yet were rare or non-existent in other countries –

and vice versa. I meticulously recorded these differences, creating a growing catalog of German peculiarities.

A Catalog of German Behaviors

One example: As a child, it was completely normal for me to wait at a red light – even if there was no car in sight. But abroad, this picture changed. It seemed perfectly natural to cross the street at a red light as long as there was no car nearby. Back in Germany, I again realized that his behavior is not accepted. The critical looks and comments reminded me how important rules are in German culture.

These observations helped me to recognize the often invisible, yet deeply ingrained behavioral rules that shape our value culture. The constant comparison with other cultures allowed me to understand not only the peculiarities of other nations but above all those of my own.

Interviews and Insights

In addition to my own observations, I conducted many interviews with Germans and people living in Germany. I asked questions like:

- What do you notice about Germans?
- What do you appreciate about German culture?
- What behaviors do you find particularly striking or strange in other countries?

The answers were diverse and opened up new perspectives for me. They confirmed some of my own observations but also brought to light aspects that had previously escaped me.

6. CULTURAL DIAGNOSIS OF GERMAN VALUE CULTURE

The System of German Value Culture

These conversations provided me with valuable insights, which I condensed into a code of conduct and continuously developed. This eventually resulted in a comprehensive system of 64 guiding values that make up German value culture. These can be summarized in 17 basic principles that form the foundation of the value culture.

Here is a brief overview of these 17 basic principles:

- Social Responsibility
- Pluralism
- Feminism
- Sincerity
- Peacefulness
- Discipline and Obedience
- Accuracy
- Work Ethic
- Love of Nature
- Sustainability
- Loyalty
- Knowledge Society
- Love of Freedom
- Personal Responsibility
- Good Manners
- Western Alliances
- Democratic Foundation

6. CULTURAL DIAGNOSIS OF GERMAN VALUE CULTURE

From Values to Rules of Conduct: The Essence of Guiding Culture

These values are reflected in concrete rules of conduct. For each value, there are numerous rules that shape everyday life. In total, we are talking about thousands of rules of conduct that belong to German culture.

Let's dive into the fascinating world of German value culture and discover what makes Germany so successful!

7. SOCIAL RESPONSIBILITY

In Germany, social responsibility is deeply ingrained in the culture and is considered an invisible bond that holds society together. The idea that everyone is jointly responsible for the well-being of the community has a long tradition.

Germany played a central role in the emergence of socialist and communist ideas. As early as 1848, Karl Marx and Friedrich Engels founded communism, which strongly advocated for social balance. Since then, there have always been political movements in Germany aimed at justice and equality.

A significant milestone was the introduction of social insurance by Otto von Bismarck in the 19th century. Germany was the first country in the world to create a comprehensive social system that included health, accident, disability, and old-age insurance. This system laid the foundation for modern social security and continues to shape the German understanding of social responsibility to this day.

All this shows how closely the well-being of the individual is linked to that of the community in Germany. We can therefore conclude that the German soul is very social. Look forward to exciting insights into the following values:

- **Respect for human dignity:** The inalienable dignity of each individual as the foundation of our coexistence.
- **Protection of the weak:** Standing up for children, the elderly, people with disabilities, and pregnant women.
- **Willingness to help:** From small everyday gestures to major commitment to volunteer work and donations.
- **Moral courage:** The courage to stand up for what is right and to take action against injustice and violence.

- **Welcome culture:** Germany's generous treatment of refugees and migrants.

7.1. Respect for Human Dignity

The principle "Die Würde des Menschen ist unantastbar" ("Human dignity shall be inviolable") stands at the forefront of the German Constitution as Article 1, Paragraph 1 and forms the foundation of German coexistence.

For Germans, this principle means that every human being, regardless of origin, ethnicity, religion, social status, gender, sexual orientation, or other personal characteristics, possesses an inalienable dignity. This dignity is also not tied to performance or success, but a fundamental human right that everyone is entitled to from birth.

This conviction obliges Germans to treat every person with respect and dignity, regardless of whether they know them, like them, or are similar to them. It reminds them that all are part of a common human family and that every individual is valuable and worthy of protection.

Empathy and Respect in Everyday Life: The Golden Rule

The proverb "Was du nicht willst, dass man dir tut, das füg' auch keinem anderen zu" ("Do unto others as you would have them do unto you") is deeply rooted in Germany and serves as a moral compass for Germans' actions. This golden rule applies to everyone, regardless of social status or role in society. Whether it's the waiter in the restaurant, the delivery driver bringing a package, or the colleague who supports you at work — everyone deserves respect and appreciation.

This is not the case in all countries. In many parts of the world, deep hierarchies are firmly anchored in society, distinguishing people according to their status or even their caste.

I experienced a particularly impressive example in India when I was a guest of a wealthy businessman. Every morning, his chauffeur drove us from his estate to his office. As soon as he got out, all the employees instantly got up and remained standing until he had crossed the room. Some rushed to him to kneel down and touch his feet. While he showed me, a foreign entrepreneur, great respect, his own staff received little recognition.

In Germany, such a strict distinction based on status would be unimaginable; Germans firmly believe that every person – regardless of their position – should be treated with the same respect.

Another proverb that illustrates their attitude is: „Beurteile einen Menschen nicht danach, wie er sich gegenüber seinen Vorgesetzten verhält, sondern danach, wie er mit denen umgeht, die ihm unterlegen sind." ("Judge a person not by how they treat their superiors, but by how they treat those who are inferior to them.") This shows that Germans understand that true greatness lies in how one treats those who depend on support.

Historical and Economic Roots

The appreciation that Germans show towards people who work for them or are less privileged has historical and economic roots. Unlike some other European countries, Germany was never a slave-holding society, so the idea of considering people as property was alien to them.

7. SOCIAL RESPONSIBILITY

Germany's economic development also played a role. The reconstruction after the Second World War and the subsequent economic miracle led to widespread prosperity and comparatively low inequality. Of course, there are differences between rich and poor in Germany as well, but compared to many other countries, the gap is less pronounced.

Appreciation of Work

As employers, Germans are committed to fair working conditions and respectful treatment of employees. They know that satisfied employees are more motivated and productive, which ultimately benefits the company's success.

But it's about more than just economic efficiency. Germans believe that every person deserves respect, regardless of whether they are in a management position or perform a so-called "simple" job.

They show this appreciation not only to their colleagues but to everyone they encounter. Germans are known for their politeness, even towards people who work for them. A simple "please" and "thank you" is a matter of course for them, whether they are talking to a waiter, a bus driver, or a cleaning lady.

The equality of all people and respect for their dignity shape the actions of Germans in everyday life and in the world of work, contributing to a society in which every person, regardless of their origin or social status, is valued and respected.

7.2. Protecting the Vulnerable

In Germany, the principle of social responsibility goes far beyond merely recognizing human dignity. Germans feel obligated to protect and support those who need help the most.

The German proverb "Schwach ist, wer Schwächere nicht schützt"("Weak is he who does not protect the weaker") calls for solidarity and shapes everyday life, especially in dealing with children, senior citizens, people with disabilities, and pregnant women.

Children

Germans want children to grow up in a safe and loving environment. They do not hesitate to intervene when a child is in danger – whether it's helping them cross a busy street, protecting them from violence, or campaigning against child labor.

Seniors

Senior citizens enjoy respect and support because they have contributed much to society. Germans are happy to offer help when an elderly person needs support – carrying groceries, crossing the street, or getting on public transport. Doors are opened for them, and seats are offered on the bus.

People with Disabilities

Germans treat people with disabilities with respect and advocate for their inclusion. They want people with disabilities to be able to participate in social life. Obstacles are removed, and help is offered – whether it's clearing a path for a wheelchair user, supporting a hearing-impaired person in a conversation, or safely accompanying a blind person.

Pregnant Women

Pregnant women and mothers are particularly close to the hearts of Germans. They offer support – carrying bags or helping them manage everyday life.

I recently experienced this at the train station: A woman was struggling to carry her stroller up the stairs. Before I could intervene, another person was already helping her. That's how it is in Germany: People help each other.

Protecting the vulnerable is a central component of German value culture. Germany is a society that cares for one another and where everyone, regardless of their abilities or life situation, has a place.

7.3. Altruism

German culture is deeply marked by respect for human dignity, which motivates Germans to protect and support the vulnerable. But their altruism goes even further, as they know that everyone, regardless of strength or weakness, needs help in certain situations.

Everyday Gestures of Altruism

In everyday life, there are many opportunities to show altruism, and Germans seize them. They take the time to explain directions to a confused tourist, even if they are in a hurry. I have seen them translate for someone who doesn't understand the language or help someone use a ticket machine.

They also lend a hand when someone needs support – whether it's carrying heavy objects, repairing a bicycle, or helping someone move.

Neighborly Altruism: A Strong Network

Altruism is particularly strong in the neighborhood. Here, where people know and trust each other, they help each other out.

It goes far beyond watering flowers during vacations: People help each other with small repairs around the house, lend tools or ingredients for cooking, look after children, or walk the dog when someone is unavailable. This neighborly solidarity creates valuable cohesion in an increasingly individualized world.

Volunteering: Altruism in Action

Volunteering is a matter of course for Germans. They are involved in many areas: They coach youth teams in sports clubs, help out at homeless shelters, work for the volunteer fire department, support refugees, or advocate for the environment. And they do all this without pay, simply to do something good.

Donations: Generosity as an Expression of Altruism

Germans also like to donate money. They support charitable organizations and projects that are important to them. Whether it's for disaster relief, education projects, or animal welfare – they like to give to help and make the world a little better.

7.4. Zivilcourage

Zivilcourage – a German word so unique that it hardly has an equivalent in English. It means "Courage in the face of social injustice". It is the rebellion of the German soul against injustice and violence, manifesting itself in courageous deeds.

Germans believe that each individual has the responsibility to stand up for a just and safe society and are not willing to stand idly by when their values are disregarded. They act, even when it is uncomfortable, and even when it could bring personal disadvantages.

Zivilcourage Against Discrimination: A Shield for the Vulnerable

Germans particularly demonstrate Zivilcourage when it comes to discrimination and racism. They do not tolerate injustice based on origin, language, disability, or religion. They stand protectively in front of the victims of racist attacks and raise their voices against hatred and intolerance.

I remember a situation when I was boarding a plane in Italy and witnessed a disgusting scene. A group of Italian football fans were vilely insulting a young man of African descent because of his skin color. The other passengers looked away, the flight attendants remained silent. I couldn't help myself. I sat down next to the young man and told the football fans to stop their insults. I started a conversation with the man to show him that he is not alone and that there are people who will stand up for him. It was a small act of German Zivilcourage and showed me how important it is to take a stand when others look away.

Zivilcourage Against Violence: Courage Against Brutality

Germans do not look away from violence and crime either. They intervene when they see someone being attacked, try to de-escalate the situation, and call the police. They are willing to put themselves in danger to help others and stop violence.

As a young boy, I witnessed an incident with my father that I still remember to this day. We saw a fight between two young men, surrounded by a cheering crowd. My father did not hesitate for a second. He went straight towards the fight while I anxiously tugged at his hand and begged him to stop. But he was undeterred and separated the two brawlers. He later explained to me that it is our responsibility to stop violence and injustice. These words have shaped me and always remind me to be courageous and stand up for what is right.

For Germans, Zivilcourage is an attitude towards life. They take responsibility for their fellow human beings and advocate for a society in which justice, security, and respect for all prevail. They are willing to stand up for their values, even if it takes courage and overcoming oneself.

7.5. Welcome Culture

The "Willkommenskultur" (welcome culture) represents Germany's commitment to welcoming refugees and migrants, offering them the opportunity to integrate into society. The term gained prominence during the 2015 refugee crisis when Germany accepted over a million refugees from Syria, Afghanistan, Iraq, and other crisis regions. Since then, Germany has welcomed over 7 million migrants in total, demonstrating its willingness to take responsibility in global humanitarian crises.

7. SOCIAL RESPONSIBILITY

Welcome Culture in Action

The "welcome culture" is not only reflected in political decisions but also in the warm reception many Germans extended to arriving refugees. In 2015, thousands of Germans lined train stations to greet refugees with gifts and open arms. Similarly, in 2022, when a large number of Ukrainian refugees arrived in Germany, many Germans spontaneously offered their homes to provide shelter. Moreover, Ukrainian refugees in Germany receive financial support that is unmatched in any other country.

Numerous civil society initiatives and organizations make significant contributions to supporting refugees. Local communities organize accommodation, donations, and volunteer work to help newcomers settle in.

This culture made the outcry in 2024 all the more significant when a video went viral showing a celebration in a posh restaurant where a group of young people sang the song "L'amour toujours" by Gigi D'Agostino – but with the shocking lyrics "Germany for the Germans, foreigners out!" The media response was overwhelming, and public outrage was enormous. How could it be that apparently well-off young people were singing such nationalistic and xenophobic lyrics? The consequences were swift: Two of those involved lost their jobs, and a young woman was denied access to her university.

This incident and the strong reaction to it highlight how deeply ingrained the welcome culture is in Germany and that xenophobia has no place in the country.

Two Types of Welcoming Culture: Heart vs. Head

Germany is fundamentally a country with a welcome culture, but there are two different approaches: an idealistic one and a rational one.

Idealism (Heart): Open Arms for the World

The idealistic welcome culture is characterized by deep humanism and a belief in universal human dignity. It dreams of a world without borders, where every person, regardless of origin, has the same right to a good life.

Proponents of this view advocate for a generous acceptance of refugees and migrants. They emphasize the moral obligation to help people in need and see diversity as an enrichment for society. They are willing to invest financial resources to promote integration and offer newcomers a perspective in Germany.

The Rational Welcoming Culture (Head): Sustainability

In contrast, the rational welcome culture acknowledges Germany's limited resources and capabilities. This perspective emphasizes the need to manage available resources responsibly and ensure that aid reaches those who need it most.

A comparison illustrates this: A migrant costs Germany a total of about 14,000 EUR per year. These funds only secure a minimum standard of living in Germany. In many countries of origin, comparable support could be provided with less than 1,400 EUR annually - i.e., for a tenth of the cost. With the same budget, one could thus help ten times as many people locally. Representatives of the rational welcome culture, therefore, argue that it is more sustainable to provide support in the countries of origin to help more people.

In addition, many in this camp find it problematic that in some federal states more than 65% of those receiving citizen's allowance have a migration background and almost 50% of total social spending goes to non-Germans.

While in Germany a significant portion of social aid is allocated to foreigners, in most other countries, non-citizens are not entitled to receive such benefits. For instance, undocumented migrants in the U.S. are ineligible for programs like Medicaid (except for Emergency Medicaid), Supplemental Nutrition Assistance Program (SNAP), Supplemental Security Income (SSI), Children's Health Insurance Program (CHIP), and Housing Assistance Programs.

The only support they might receive comes from a few states like California and New York, which offer limited assistance to specific groups of non-citizens. This means that most migrants in the U.S. come to work and contribute to the country's economic growth. In contrast, many migrants in Germany seek generous financial aid without having to work, a fact that Germans may find challenging despite their welcome culture.

The rational welcome culture sees Germany as a large family. As in any family, the basic needs of all family members – i.e., Germans – must be met first. Only when food, education, work, and healthcare are secured can one comprehensively care for people from other countries.

Moreover, the rational welcome culture favors self-help over external help. The principle is comparable to the safety instructions on an airplane: In the event of a loss of cabin pressure, you put on your own oxygen mask first before helping others. Why? Because if you get no oxygen, you won't be able to help others! Similarly, only a strong and stable society can effectively help others. An overwhelmed society, on the other hand, can neither do justice to its own citizens nor to newcomers.

This perspective advocates prioritizing the admission of refugees who face genuine political persecution in their home countries. A key point of emphasis is ensuring that migrants are truly in need of protection and preventing any abuse of the asylum system.

One major concern is the tactic used by some migrants who discard their passports upon arrival to make false claims about their age or origin. For instance, a 25-year-old migrant from Turkey might claim to be only 16 and from war-torn Syria. Despite legitimate doubts, authorities often have no choice but to accept these statements without thorough verification. Medical age assessments can only be carried out with the migrant's consent. A review in Lower Saxony found that, out of 157 supposed "minors," nearly 60% were actually adults.

In addition to these issues, there's growing alarm over cases of social welfare fraud among some refugees. While German citizens must provide identification and disclose their assets to receive welfare, the same strict requirements often don't apply to non-Germans. This loophole has allowed foreign nationals, even those with substantial wealth abroad, to receive welfare benefits in Germany.

Another widespread issue involves refugees exploiting the system by claiming welfare under multiple identities. In some cases, migrants present different identities to different authorities—or even the same authority but with altered appearances—to collect benefits multiple times. One extreme example is a Somali refugee who received social welfare 14 times every month using 14 different identities like Kash A., Bahr A. and Ali A.. Each identity received payments, which he withdrew from ATMs using various bank accounts.

This rational welcome culture is not an expression of heartlessness, but of responsibility and pragmatism. It seeks a sustainable way to help people in need without jeopardizing the stability and well-being of one's own society.

Regardless of whether one takes the idealistic or rational view, one thing remains clear: Everyone who comes to Germany is treated well. The welcome culture shows Germany's willingness to help people in need and is an expression of humanity and compassion.

8. PLURALISM

Pluralism encompasses the acceptance of diverse ways of life, the promotion of diversity and tolerance, and the active fight against discrimination. This principle creates a society where everyone – regardless of origin, religion, or lifestyle – finds their place.

In Germany, people of various ethnicities, religions, and lifestyles live together, all contributing to the vibrant dynamism of society. However, this diversity also brings challenges, as cultural differences often lead to misunderstandings. Pluralism strives to overcome these differences and strengthen respect for diversity.

In this chapter, we delve deeper into pluralism and explore how it shapes the lives of Germans:

- **Respect for Diversity and Tolerance:** How Germany, learning from the lessons of the past, has developed a strong respect for diversity and decisively combats discrimination.
- **Sexual Freedom:** The importance of acceptance and appreciation of individual freedom regarding sexual orientation and gender identity.
- **Religious Freedom:** A deep-rooted tradition that forms the foundation for peaceful coexistence in Germany.
- **Fight Against Anti-Semitism:** The unwavering commitment to combating anti-Semitism and protecting Jewish life.

8. PLURALISM

8.1. Diversity and Tolerance

German society places great value on diversity and tolerance. The cruel experiences of the past, particularly the horrors of the Nazi regime, have taught Germany an indelible lesson: discrimination and hatred lead to unspeakable suffering.

The Legacy of National Socialism

During the Nazi regime, people were systematically discriminated against and persecuted based on racist ideologies. The Nazis propagated the superiority of the "Aryan race" and implemented a policy of dehumanization and terror. Laws like the Nuremberg Laws of 1935 stripped Jews of their civil rights, while the euthanasia program claimed the lives of people with disabilities. Homosexuals and other minorities were persecuted, imprisoned, and deported to concentration camps.

From this dark past arises Germany's obligation to protect the rights of all people and ensure that such atrocities never happen again.

Diversity as an Enrichment of Society

Today, people of different origins, religions, and lifestyles are met with openness and respect in Germany. Diversity is not only tolerated but seen as a valuable enrichment. Racism and exclusion are decisively rejected in Germany. Discrimination based on skin color, religion, gender, or sexual orientation is not tolerated. Whether in private settings, at work, or in public – racism and discrimination are actively countered.

Subtle Discrimination

Despite all the progress in terms of tolerance and inclusion, subtle forms of discrimination still exist in some areas. People are sometimes disadvantaged or confronted with prejudice based on their ethnic origin or nationality.

An example of this can be found in dating behavior: In dating apps in Germany, men from Western countries like the USA, Germany, France, or Sweden are often preferred, while men from Eastern Europe or the Middle East, for example from Ukraine, Poland, Romania, Or Syria, Lebanon or Iraq face greater challenges due to their origin. This hidden discrimination shows that unconscious biases and stereotypes still exist.

A Polish friend told me how he had been in contact with a German woman for a long time who, because of his accent, thought he was American. However, when she found out that he was from Poland, she abruptly lost interest.

Another friend from Germany, whose parents were from Russia, reported that he faced prejudice simply because of his name "Igor." To avoid this, he changed his name to "Leonard," and the prejudice disappeared. Such examples show that subtle forms of discrimination are still present in Germany.

Diversity in the Workplace

German employers actively strive for diversity in their teams by hiring people with different backgrounds and identities to create an inclusive work environment. Diversity strengthens collaboration and promotes creative solutions and innovation.

8. PLURALISM

Despite these efforts, however, prejudice persists, particularly regarding leadership positions. Many employers still prefer applicants with German citizenship for management roles.

Several friends from Eastern Europe and South Asia told me that after studying in Germany, they found jobs but were passed over for promotions. They felt there was a "glass ceiling" and that their German employers did not see them as suitable leaders. Disappointed, they returned to their home countries, where they quickly advanced their careers and reached leadership positions. This shows that while many Germans officially reject discrimination, they are still unconsciously influenced by nationality or ethnicity.

Racism: A Problem That Needs to be Addressed

Racism exists in Germany, but it is less pronounced than in many other parts of the world. In China, for example, it would not be uncommon for a taxi driver to say to me: "You're German. I like Germans." And then add, "But there are too many Africans here. I would never give a ride to someone like that, and none of my colleagues pick up Black people."

Even some of my Asian friends, who studied at a prestigious university, were shocked when they had a marketing professor from Argentina. When I asked what was wrong with the professor and whether it had to do with his qualifications, they responded: "No, but he's from Argentina. Argentina is poorer than China. What can we learn from him?"

This type of open discrimination, which is commonplace in many countries, is fortunately rare in Germany. However, even in Germany, there are still prejudices deeply rooted in the subconscious, although Germany strives to treat everyone without prejudice and judge them based on their individual abilities.

Different Perspectives on Tolerance

Despite the broad consensus in Germany regarding the importance of tolerance, there are different perspectives: the conservative-tolerant and the progressive-tolerant.

Conservative-Tolerant: Tolerance with the Rule of Law

The conservative-tolerant believe that everyone should have the right to think and act as they wish, as long as they do not harm anyone. They are open to everyone, regardless of skin color, religion, sexual orientation, or political opinion. The only intolerance they allow concerns violations of the law. For them, the rule of law is of central importance despite all tolerance. Therefore, in their opinion, illegal immigrants should be deported – not because of their origin, but to preserve the integrity of the rule of law.

Progressive Tolerance: Tolerance Through Exclusion?

The progressive-tolerant perspective often views conservative tolerance as a hidden form of intolerance, particularly concerning illegal immigrants. This stance is frequently interpreted as containing biases that could enable ethnic or religious discrimination. In pursuit of a truly tolerant society, many progressive advocates argue that conservative voices should be excluded from major social institutions and media platforms. Their rationale: genuine tolerance requires showing intolerance toward intolerant attitudes.

8. PLURALISM

I saw an example of this stance in the case of an acquaintance who was excluded from a labor union solely because he openly declared his membership in a political party, the AfD, which politically is similar to the MAGA movement in the USA.

Yet, all Germans share the goal of a tolerant coexistence and acceptance of diversity. Society has grown from the mistakes of the past and continues to strive toward an inclusive community where each person—regardless of background or personal beliefs—is respected and valued.

8.2. Sexual Freedom

Acceptance and respect are core values in Germany, and this is also reflected in the approach to sexual orientation and gender identity. The individual freedom to live one's own sexuality and identity is highly valued. Discrimination or insults based on these characteristics are totally rejected.

An Evolution of Cultural Values

German society has undergone a significant shift towards greater acceptance of sexual diversity in recent years. While the traditional image of monogamous marriage between a man and a woman is still present, openness towards other relationship models and sexual orientations has increased. Homosexuality and bisexuality are now largely accepted, and many prominent figures openly talk about their sexual orientation.

The legal recognition of transgender people has also progressed. In Germany, it is possible to change one's gender in the civil registry without the need for medical interventions or a court decision. The decisions of transgender people regarding their lived gender are respected, and their preferred pronouns are used. Using the wrong form of address can be perceived as disrespectful in Germany, while using the correct form contributes to an inclusive and respectful coexistence.

Different Perspectives on Sexual Freedom: Ideologues vs. Liberals

Despite these developments, there are different views on sexuality in Germany, which can be roughly divided into two camps: the ideologues and the liberals.

Ideologues: Sexual Freedom Above All

The ideologues argue that despite legal equality, discrimination still exists. They advocate for increased visibility and promotion of LGBTQ+ to break down prejudices. This also includes educating children about these topics at an early age to prevent prejudice.

They demand that changing one's gender in official documents should be quick and uncomplicated and that transgender people should be allowed to use restrooms and participate in sports according to their gender identity. They also advocate for children who wish to do so to have access to hormone therapies or surgical interventions at an early age.

Liberals: No Imposition of Sexuality

The German liberals (people valuing freedom, not to be confused with the US American "Liberals") also believe that everyone has the right to live their sexuality freely. However, they believe that intimacy belongs in the private sphere and that sexual topics should be treated discreetly in public, regardless of whether they involve homo- or heterosexual relationships.

In their view, topics like homosexuality and transsexuality should be introduced in schools during adolescence, as they believe that early childhood education on these subjects is primarily the responsibility of parents and should not begin in kindergarten.

They also advocate for the protection of biological women in areas such as sports and public facilities. Concerns have arisen regarding cases in the U.S. where some heterosexual men have changed their gender to compete in women's sports, potentially gaining access to lucrative prize money or scholarships.

Additionally, there is concern that male offenders could change their gender to be placed in women's prisons. A recent example in Scotland illustrates this issue: a convicted rapist, who had lived his entire life as a man and was convicted of assaulting two women, declared shortly before sentencing that he identified as a woman and was subsequently assigned to a women's prison. The resulting protests were so intense that even Scotland's First Minister Nicola Sturgeon faced calls to step down.

Many migrants and Germans with a migration background share the views of the German liberals and are cautious about the LGBTQ+ movement. They prefer traditional family values and are critical of the increasing liberalization of sexuality. These groups advocate for more discretion in dealing with sexual topics in public and a restrained approach to early childhood education.

Despite differing views, there is a broad consensus in Germany that sexuality is a private matter. This attitude fosters a climate of respect and tolerance in which everyone's privacy is respected.

8.3. Religious Freedom

In Germany, religious freedom is a central value for peaceful coexistence in a multicultural society. This right is not only enshrined in the constitution but also shapes public and private life. It allows everyone to freely express their religious identity without fear of persecution or discrimination.

The Constitution as Guarantor of Religious Freedom

The German Constitution, created after the horrors of World War II, draws lessons from a past in which religious intolerance led to great suffering. Article 4 unequivocally guarantees religious freedom:

Freedom of faith and of conscience, and freedom to profess a religious or philosophical creed, shall be inviolable. The undisturbed practice of religion shall be guaranteed.

These words are not only legal safeguards but also an obligation of society to grant everyone the freedom to choose, practice, or change their religion.

Historical Roots and Significance for the Present

The Reformation in the 16th century, led by Martin Luther, resulted in a break with the Roman Catholic Church and religious conflicts that shook the Holy Roman Empire. The Thirty Years' War (1618–1648) ended with the Peace of Westphalia, which laid the foundation for tolerance towards different denominations.

8. PLURALISM

The Weimar Constitution of 1919 guaranteed religious freedom for the first time and separated church and state. But these achievements were destroyed during the Nazi dictatorship (1933–1945) when religious minorities, especially Jews, were systematically persecuted. This dark past led to an unwavering commitment to religious freedom after World War II.

Religious Freedom in Everyday Life

Today, religious freedom in Germany is reflected in the diversity of everyday life. In many cities, synagogues, mosques, churches, and temples often exist side by side. The construction of new places of worship, including synagogues and mosques, is encouraged to ensure that every religious community can freely practice their religion.

Regular interreligious dialogues also promote respect and understanding between different faiths.

Respect for Religious Symbols

It's a sign of our times: Even people who don't belong to any religion treat religious symbols with respect. Whether it's a cross necklace, a headscarf, or a kippah – these symbols of faith are valued as part of a colorful mosaic where everyone can freely express their identity.

And it's not just the symbols; the central figures of religions like Muhammad, Jesus, or Buddha are also respected in Germany. An example of this is the wave of indignation triggered by a disrespectful depiction of the "Last Supper" at the 2024 Olympic Games in Paris. Freedom of expression may be a right in Germany, but many wondered: Did public funds really need to be used for this?

Negative Religious Freedom

In Germany, religious freedom also means the right not to belong to any religion. This negative religious freedom guarantees that atheists and agnostics enjoy the same respect and protection as believers.

By respecting religious freedom, Germany promotes a society based on respect and humanity. Religious freedom forms the core of a peaceful and just society where everyone finds their place – regardless of faith or non-belief.

8.4. Combating Anti-Semitism

Anti-Semitism is a poison that is not tolerated under any circumstances in Germany. The country pursues a policy of absolute zero tolerance towards any form of anti-Semitic behavior.

The Indelible Scar of the Holocaust

The memory of the Holocaust, in which millions of Jews were systematically murdered, is deeply ingrained in the national consciousness. Germany bears the heavy burden of collective guilt for these unspeakable crimes and vows that such a breach of civilization must never happen again. With all determination, Germany combats the denial or trivialization of these historical facts and promotes awareness of the horrors of the past through education, memorials, and museums.

Jewish Life in Germany

Before the rise of National Socialism, Germany was a place where Jewish life flourished. Jewish citizens were firmly integrated into society and made significant contributions to the country's cultural and economic prosperity. Just think of figures like Albert Einstein or the Rothschild family.

The deep connection between Jews and non-Jews in Germany is also evident in the fact that in the 1920s and 1930s, around 30% of Jewish marriages were with non-Jews.

Active Resistance to Anti-Semitism

Today, Germany is once again a country where Jews feel safe. But unfortunately, there are signs of a resurgence of anti-Semitism, which is why Germans think it is crucial to remain vigilant and actively combat any form of hostility towards Jews.

In right-wing circles, there are still Holocaust deniers and spreaders of hate propaganda. On the left, Israel is often demonized, and anti-Zionism sometimes turns into anti-Semitism, especially when anti-Jewish stereotypes are used or the Israeli government is compared to the Nazi regime.

Also worrying is anti-Semitism among migrants, particularly from Muslim-majority countries, where hostility towards Jews is often deeply rooted. On my travels through the Middle East and North Africa, I have witnessed how openly hatred of Jews is expressed there. People even praised the German crimes of World War II and downplayed the Holocaust. People sometimes came to me and said: "You are from Germany! We like Germany. Germany was the only country that was able to effectively work against the Jews". These prejudices are often brought to Germany and lead to anti-Semitic incidents here.

Of particular concern is the increase in anti-Semitic crimes, which has further intensified after the Hamas attack on Israel on October 7, 2023, and the subsequent Israeli military intervention. Since then, many Jews in Germany have felt increasingly threatened, especially when they publicly display their Jewish identity by wearing symbols such as the kippah or the Star of David.

A particularly sensational case was that of the Jewish musician Gil Ofarim, who claimed to have been discriminated against in a hotel because of a chain with a Star of David. These accusations triggered great outrage and calls for a boycott of the hotel. Later, however, it turned out that Ofarim had fabricated the accusations. Nevertheless, this incident clearly showed how sensitive the issue of anti-Semitism is in Germany and that any form of hostility towards Jews is decisively combated.

The fight against anti-Semitism concerns the whole of society. Germany must not allow anti-Semitism to become socially acceptable again. The Jewish community is an indispensable part of Germany, and its protection is a top priority. Synagogues, Jewish schools, and other institutions are protected by comprehensive security measures.

Germans see it as their responsibility to actively combat anti-Semitic tendencies, to not leave conspiracy theories and hate speech unanswered and to stand up against anti-Semitic aggression.

9. FEMINISM

The history of feminism in Germany is a story of struggle, progress, and continuous development. From the first courageous women who took to the streets for their right to vote to today's debates about gender quotas and identity politics – the road to equality has been long and paved with numerous challenges.

But equality is much more than just a paragraph in a law. It is about ensuring that women can live their everyday lives free from discrimination and prejudice.

Look forward to exciting insights into:

- **Equality:** The historical milestones of feminism and the current challenges on the path to a truly equal society.
- **Protection of Women:** How women are protected from violence and discrimination in Germany.
- **Respect for Women:** How this respect manifests itself in everyday life, interpersonal relationships, and public life.

9.1. Gender Equality

While it is now taken for granted in Germany that women enjoy the same rights as men, this achievement is the result of a long and arduous struggle. From the first courageous women who took to the streets for their right to vote to today's debates about gender quotas and identity politics – the road to equality has been long and paved with numerous challenges.

Milestones on the Path to Equality

In 1918, shortly after the end of World War I, women's suffrage was introduced in Germany. This made Germany one of the pioneers in Europe. Women not only received the right to vote but also the right to stand for political office. This was a decisive turning point in German history.

The Equal Rights Act followed in 1958, ending the husband's guardianship and giving women full economic independence. Finally, they could independently conclude contracts and dispose of their own income. This progress made Germany a pioneer in Europe, as comparable laws only came into force in France in 1965, in Italy in 1975, and in Spain in 1981. Germany thus showed early on that gender equality is of great importance.

From Legal Equality to Lived Reality

Although women are now legally equal, the path to actual equality is not yet complete, even in Germany. Prejudices and discriminatory behaviors are still deeply rooted. One example: A small driving error in traffic, and immediately one hears the mocking comment: "Typisch Frau." ("Typical woman.") A phrase that cements decades-old stereotypes, even though studies show that women drive more safely and defensively.

When women rise to leadership positions, whispers often follow: "Did she sleep her way to the top?" – as if they could not have achieved their success through hard work and competence. Even Angela Merkel, the first female chancellor, had to deal with comments that she only eliminated her male competitors through political skill. This raises the question:

9. FEMINISM

Doesn't everyone who wants to become chancellor have to master the rules of the political game?

So in the minds of some Germans full gender equality has not yet arrived.

Active Promotion and Lived Equality

Germany is actively committed to ensuring that women have the same opportunities as men in all areas of life. In leadership positions, with equal pay for equal work, and in male-dominated sectors such as STEM fields, they promote women and encourage them to freely develop their talents. Programs to promote women in management and technical professions are now firmly established.

Public Space: Together Instead of Separate

Women and men also encounter each other as equal partners in public life. Apart from gender-separated restrooms to protect privacy, they share space – in churches, schools, sports, and public transport. This is seen as a sign of an egalitarian society.

Traditional vs. Modern Feminism

However, there are different views on feminism in Germany. Traditional feminism advocates for equal rights and equal opportunities and is satisfied with the progress made. Modern feminism, on the other hand, demands equal representation of women in all important positions, sometimes through gender quotas.

This focus on gender distribution—often referred to as identity politics—has led to the intentional preference for women in certain sectors. In both business and politics, female applicants are often favored over their male counterparts with similar qualifications to increase female representation. This "positive" discrimination means that women, in some areas, enjoy certain advantages over male colleagues.

For example, it has become evident that female startup founders may find it easier to attract investors or media attention. Even my feminist friends who have launched startups acknowledge this trend. Numerous public support programs and private investment funds explicitly back female-led enterprises, reinforcing this tendency. In the startup scene, male founders now often seek female co-founders to enhance their chances of securing funding.

This explicit preference for women has left many men feeling discriminated against. While men remain overrepresented in various professions, being male can be a distinct disadvantage for individual candidates. The original goal of equality policies—to reduce disadvantages—now risks creating new discrimination.

For the majority in Germany, equality means that all genders should have the same rights without rigid quotas. It is acknowledged that differences between men and women exist, and a 50-50 distribution is not realistic in all professions. The important thing is that each person, regardless of gender, is judged on their abilities.

Despite differing opinions on the degree of support for women, Germans agree that women should have the same rights and opportunities as men.

9.2. Protection of Women

In Germany, gender equality is firmly established, and men and women are generally treated equally. However, Germans also understand that equality does not mean turning a blind eye to realities. They recognize that women need special protection and consideration in certain situations and act accordingly.

Sexual Offenses: An Attack on the Soul of Society

Sexual assault is abhorred in Germany and is considered an attack on a person's dignity. Germans prosecute these crimes with the full force of the law. There are no gray areas: any sexual act without clear consent is rape, regardless of the victim's condition.

The case of the 15-year-old girl in Hamburg who was the victim of a gang rape deeply shocked the country. When only one of the ten perpetrators had to go to prison and the others were released on probation, there was a public outcry. Germans will not stand idly by when women are victimized, because the protection of women's physical and mental integrity is non-negotiable for them.

The increase in rapes of women is also extremely worrying for Germans. In 2023, almost 10,000 women were raped, which corresponds to about 300 cases per day. North Rhine-Westphalia, the most populous federal state, was particularly affected, with 3,385 cases, including 240 gang rapes.

Particularly alarming is the fact that over half of these crimes were committed by non-Germans, with more than 65% of the perpetrators having a migration background. These figures have sparked outrage in Germany, as many citizens view the increase in such incidents as a direct threat to women's safety.

Although Germans generally value their welcoming culture, the protection of women's physical and emotional well-being is non-negotiable. It is the deep-seated aversion to violence against women that has significantly shifted German attitudes toward migration, making them notably less positive than they were ten years ago.

A Safe Environment for Women

If women are harassed in public, Germans do not hesitate to intervene, reprimand the perpetrator, and seek help if necessary. They want women to feel safe and respected in Germany.

Domestic Violence: The Invisible Enemy

Domestic violence is particularly insidious because it often happens behind closed doors. If Germans notice signs of domestic violence, they offer support and inform the police if necessary. It is a balancing act between respecting privacy and the obligation to help people in need.

A dense network of aid organizations, counseling centers, and women's shelters offers affected women protection, psychological care, and legal advice. Violence against women is not tolerated under any circumstances in Germany. Relationship problems such as infidelity or financial difficulties are no excuse for violence.

Protecting women is a central priority in Germany. Society is actively committed to ensuring that women live in an environment where violence has no place.

9.3. Respect for Women

In Germany, respect for personal boundaries, especially towards women, is sacrosanct. Germans are aware of their responsibility to treat women with respect and consideration and actively ensure a safe and comfortable environment for all.

Ladies First: More Than Just Etiquette

This appreciation for women is already evident in everyday courtesy rules. The principle of "Ladies first" is deeply rooted in German culture and goes beyond mere etiquette. In Germany, "Ladies first" does not just mean holding doors open or giving women precedence; it is a sign of recognition and consideration.

In everyday life, Germans demonstrate this in various ways: in restaurants, men hold the door open for women; at social events, they offer them the preferred seat; and on crowded subways, they naturally give up their seats. If a woman is struggling with heavy bags or her car breaks down, they are happy to help. These gestures may seem old-fashioned, but they are an expression of a culture that values and protects women.

Harassment: An Absolute No-Go

Following, harassing, or even touching women is an absolute taboo in Germany and is considered not only disrespectful but also potentially criminal. Any form of sexual approach, whether verbal or physical, is strictly prohibited.

Especially in crowded public transport, Germans are careful not to crowd women and to keep a sufficient distance. Even if a woman wears tight-fitting or revealing clothing, this is never an invitation for intrusive glances or even touching.

The attacks on New Year's Eve 2015 in Cologne, where hundreds of women were victims of sexual harassment and violence, raised social awareness of this issue. They served as a stark reminder of how important it is to protect women from such attacks and create a climate where they can feel safe at all times.

Unfortunately, even in Germany, it is a sad reality that women are often affected by harassment, which leads to a feeling of insecurity for many – a situation that Germans are determined to counteract.

No Staring: Discretion is Key

An attractive woman may naturally catch the eye of a German, but this is not shown by intrusive staring. Fleeting eye contact is human and normal, but prolonged staring, especially at intimate body parts, is an absolute no-go. Such behavior can make women feel uncomfortable, and Germans respect their desire for privacy.

Catcalling: Disrespect That Will Not Be Tolerated

Whistling, shouting after someone, making suggestive remarks – "catcalling" in Germany is more than just a faux pas; it is disrespect that will not be tolerated. Such behaviors create a feeling of insecurity and discomfort for the woman concerned.

Imagine you are walking down the street, and suddenly you hear a loud whistle behind you. You turn around and see a group of men grinning suggestively at you. How would you feel? Probably insecure, maybe even scared. This is precisely why catcalling is frowned upon in Germany. It crosses personal boundaries and can make public spaces unsafe for women.

If Germans want to address a woman, this only happens after clear eye contact and a positive signal from her. Even then, politeness and restraint are maintained to avoid putting the woman in an uncomfortable situation. If she shows no interest, this is accepted without discussion. A "no" means "no" – and that is respected.

No Dress Code for Women

In Germany, no one expects women to veil themselves or dress inconspicuously to avoid unwanted attention. Women have the unrestricted right to dress as they please without having to fear harassment or assault. The responsibility always lies with men to behave respectfully.

Respect for women's personal boundaries is a central value. Germans are aware of their responsibility to always act with respect and consideration.

10. SINCERITY

Honesty, directness, fairness, and reliability – these four values form the foundation of German sincerity, a cornerstone of the German identity that earns them respect worldwide.

But what is truly behind these concepts? How do they shape German everyday life, relationships, and the business world?

Look forward to exciting insights into:

- **Honesty:** The importance of truthfulness and integrity in German everyday life and business, where a handshake is worth more than a contract.
- **Directness:** The German preference for clear and open communication – not mincing words, but also not giving false praise.
- **Tax Compliance:** The German attitude towards taxes as an expression of solidarity and responsibility.
- **Fairness:** The pursuit of justice and balance in interpersonal relationships and business practices.
- **Reliability:** The high value placed on commitment and dependability in German culture – keeping promises.

10.1. Honesty

In Germany, honesty is a fundamental value upon which trust and social interaction are built.

A Handshake Stronger Than Any Contract

A well-known proverb, often attributed to Hanseatic merchants, states: "Ein Handschlag gilt mehr als ein Vertrag."

10. SINCERITY

("A handshake is worth more than a contract.") It emphasizes the importance of trustworthiness and integrity, which played a central role in German history from early on. During the Hanseatic period, merchants built a far-reaching trade network based on contractual loyalty through reliability and honest dealings. These relationships flourished because people could rely on the honesty of their partners.

Truth Above All

Germans attach great importance to always telling the truth. Even small lies that are considered harmless elsewhere are an absolute no-go here. If a woman asks her husband if she looks too fat, and he thinks so, he will answer honestly: "Yes, my dear, you are too fat." This direct statement might be considered very impolite in other countries. But a German would tell you that saying anything that is not 100% the truth is lying.

No Fake Gestures: Genuine Feelings Instead of False Friendliness

In Germany, it's about being authentic and showing genuine feelings. Put-on friendliness or artificial gestures are frowned upon. Friendliness that is not based on real feelings is disparagingly referred to as "scheißfreundlich" – a term that literally means "Shit friendly". This stands in stark contrast to many other cultures, like the U.S., where politeness often takes precedence over authentic emotions. Imagine you're a waiter at a restaurant having a rough day; in most countries, you're still expected to smile and be friendly to customers. In Germany, however, people might even be put off by a "put-on" smile, viewing it as a false emotion and preferring a natural response instead.

No Dishonest Enrichment

In Germany, honesty is not only shown in words but also in actions. Germans always pay the correct price for goods and services. If they receive too much change, they return it.

Found objects, whether a smartphone or a wallet, are either returned directly to the owner or taken to the lost and found office – without taking a single cent. Finders often receive a legally anchored finder's reward in recognition of their honesty.

Recently, while researching what distinguishes Germany from other countries, I came across testimonials from foreigners who particularly emphasized German honesty. They recounted how lost items like an iPhone and a wallet were simply returned to them by the finders. Something like that, they said, would only happen in Germany.

Self-Service Based on Trust

In many rural areas of Germany, there are unmanned stalls where you serve yourself and put the money in a provided cash box. Imagine: a small stand on the roadside with fresh eggs, flowers, or apples, no salesperson, just a sign with prices and a cash box. While this is unimagineable to many outside of Germany, this until very recently was normal in Germany.

Newspaper stands also work this way: you take a newspaper and throw the corresponding amount into the box. There is no surveillance – only trust.

10. SINCERITY

This may seem naive to people from other countries, but in Germany, these systems work surprisingly well. Most people follow the rules because they know that this is the only way the system can survive.

In Germany, honesty is not only a moral obligation but also a success factor. It creates trust, promotes cooperation, and enables efficient work without constant supervision. These values are deeply rooted in German culture and contribute to Germans being internationally valued for their reliability.

10.2. Directness

A central value in German culture is direct and open communication. Germans say what they mean, and mean what they say. Honesty and clarity often take precedence over politeness or pleasantries. Indirect or unclear communication is often perceived as insincere or even sneaky.

Plain Language Instead of Coded Messages

Problems are addressed directly instead of being swept under the rug, which creates clarity and enables quick solutions. You get straight to the point without a lot of guesswork.

I still remember my first business contacts with Chinese colleagues. Their indirect communication, where you had to read between the lines, often drove me to despair. As an advocate of directness, I demanded clear statements and was very pushy, which was not always well received. Now, I understand that few cultures value directness as much as Germans do, and expecting it can lead to misunderstandings. Instead, I've learned to appreciate the nuances of indirect communication, recognizing that sometimes, what's left unsaid speaks volumes.

Honesty and Commitment

Germans take their counterparts at their word because they only say what they really mean. In other cultures, it is common to ask about someone's well-being without expecting a real answer – more as a greeting.

When I was a student in the USA, I was often greeted with a casual "How are you?" to which I would respond in a sincere way. My detailed answers were usually met with a puzzled look and a quick "Good, thanks!" as the other person moved on. So their question felt like an empty phrase to me, without genuine interest. In Germany, on the other hand, you only ask "Wie geht's?" (how is it going) if you really want to know and expect an honest answer.

Efficiency and Focus: No Time for Small Talk

German directness also means: no detours through empty phrases or small talk, just straight to the point. Imagine: an email that starts directly with the main issue, no beating around the bush. In many cultures, unthinkable – in Germany, it's totally normal.

In countries like Brazil, communication looks very different. Even a WhatsApp message starts with a friendly "Oi, tudo bem?" ("Hey, everything good?") and a brief exchange about how everyone's doing before diving into the actual topic. My Brazilian friends have shown me that even in the digital world, you can't just jump right in. A bit of small talk is a must!

Germans, on the other hand, prefer getting efficiently to the core of things, especially in business. Small talk is allowed, but respecting the other person's time is crucial.

Constructive Criticism and Honest Praise

Directness also shows up in German feedback culture. In Germany, people get straight to the point without skirting around issues. This open, direct feedback might sometimes sound a bit harsh, but it's not meant personally.

On the other hand, praise isn't given out lightly but only when it's truly deserved. Many Germans dislike empty compliments or insincere flattery. So, if a German gives you a compliment, you can be sure it's genuine.

Clarity and Understanding

Clear statements are appreciated. If something cannot or should not be done, it is stated openly. A clear "no" is better than a vague "maybe" that creates disappointment. This directness ensures that misunderstandings are rare because everyone clearly communicates what they mean.

This German directness may seem impolite to some, but it reflects the German need for honest and clear communication. Germans believe that openness leads to better understanding and more effective collaboration.

10.3. Tax Compliance

In Germany, paying taxes honestly is more than just an obligation – it's a matter of honor and social cohesion. As taxes secure infrastructure, education, healthcare, and many other public services, everyone wants to contribute their share to the well-being of the community.

Tax Evasion: an Absolute Taboo

Tax evasion in Germany is not only illegal but also morally reprehensible. Those who evade taxes are considered unsupportive and lose not only money but also the trust and respect of society.

Tax Compliance in Retreat

While the majority of Germans fulfill their tax obligations, there is a diminishing willingness in some circles to contribute fairly to the community. In particular, wealthy elites exploit legal loopholes to evade their tax burdens. By establishing companies and foundations in tax havens, they shift their income abroad, thus minimizing their tax payments in Germany.

This practice is not uncommon. Many successful entrepreneurs and investors use such models to increase their wealth. For example, profits from online businesses are often processed through companies in Panama, where they are not subject to taxation. With this money, further investments are then made in companies or real estate. Although these individuals have their residence in Germany and are therefore generally liable for taxes, they often pay themselves only modest salaries to reduce their tax burden.

For the average citizen, who is employed by a German employer, such tax optimization strategies are unattainable. While they work hard, nearly half of their income is withheld for taxes and social contributions.

10. SINCERITY

Waste of Money: Where is the Justice?

These citizens then see how 11 billion euros flow to the American chip manufacturer Intel in government subsidy – a company that is already swimming in money. At the same time, they have to turn every penny over twice. Add to this examples like the 139,000 euros spent on stylists for Foreign Minister Annalena Baerbock – luxury at the state's expense, while many citizens struggle with rising living costs.

Development aid funds also raise questions. Peru receives 529 million euros from Germany for new cycle paths, while bridges in Germany are dilapidated and schools are overcrowded. India receives 987 million euros and has its own space program, while German research is often neglected.

Growing Frustration

It is no wonder that I meet more and more Germans abroad who report their frustration with the high tax burden, the dwindling performance mentality, and the waste of tax money. These experiences have led many high achievers to emigrate, and more and more people are following this example.

Despite this frustration, it remains to be said that a large proportion of Germans still consider their taxes to be an indispensable contribution to the common good and pay them conscientiously – an attitude that is only found in this form in a few regions of the world.

10.4. Fairness

Fairness is a deeply rooted value in Germany that shapes social interactions. It's not just about maximizing one's own advantage but also considering the interests of others and creating win-win situations.

The Honorable Merchant: A Role Model for Integrity

The concept of the "Ehrbaren Kaufmanns" ("Honorable Merchant") from the Hanseatic period embodies this ideal. Hanseatic merchants were known for their honesty, reliability, and integrity. They acted not only in their own interest but always had the well-being of their business partners and the community in mind. This ethic and these standards were the basis of the trust on which the Hanseatic trade relations were built – a legacy that continues to this day.

Fairness in Trade: Give and Take

Fairness is also reflected in setting fair prices and not demanding exorbitant ones. The deliberate exploitation of hardship to achieve inflated prices is not only morally reprehensible in Germany but also punishable by law. Section 291 of the "Strafgesetzbuch" (Criminal Code) protects consumers from exploitation and ensures fair market conditions. This regulation reflects the conviction that an honest price gives the seller fair compensation and the buyer the feeling of having made a fair deal.

Negotiations: Cooperation Instead of Confrontation

In negotiations, Germans prefer a cooperative and respectful approach. It is about listening to all parties involved and their arguments to find a solution together that is acceptable to all sides. The goal is not to outsmart or outmaneuver the negotiating partner but to create a win-win situation from which everyone benefits.

In German sales negotiations there is not much haggling. People trust that the prices quoted are fair and reasonable. However, salespeople report that foreign customers often negotiate more aggressively because they do not have the same trust in pricing. Unfortunately, this leads to some German salespeople taking a more defensive stance from the outset and being less willing to compromise when negotiating with foreign buyers.

Returning Goods: An Uneasy Feeling

Although the right of return is legally enshrined, many Germans are hesitant to exercise it – especially the older generation. A purchase is seen as a binding decision, and people think carefully about what they really need before buying to avoid unnecessary returns. My own father for example has often admonished me to only order what I really want to keep.

Germans want both sides to be treated fairly and to be satisfied in the end.

10.5. Reliability

Reliability is a core value in German culture and firmly anchored in business life. Proverbs like "Ein Mann, ein Wort" ("A man, a word") and "Was man verspricht, das hält man auch" ("What you promise, you also keep") illustrate the high importance of binding commitments.

Reliability is Not a Given Everywhere

At the beginning of my entrepreneurial journey 15 years ago, I was strongly influenced by German reliability and expected the same from international partners. So I paid in advance for software that was supposed to be ready by the agreed date – but never received it. In retrospect, I was naive, as I expected a high degree of reliability due to my German perspective.

My German friends reacted with incomprehension: "Why are you working with foreigners?" Even a Swedish friend said: "I would only work with Germans or Swedes. I wouldn't trust Asian developers." A coach at an international business meeting confirmed this picture and advised working primarily with Americans or Europeans, especially Germans, as other nations were cheaper but less reliable.

Although I reject such stereotypes, and continue to work with people across the globe, my experience with over 500 business partners and contractors has shown me that in general Germans can indeed be considered more reliable – and this reputation is internationally known.

Reliability in Everyday Life

Germans are proud that you can rely on their word – whether in professional or private life. A promise is not an empty phrase but a serious commitment. Commitments are only made if they can be kept. In everyday working life, realistic schedules are created, and delays are communicated openly.

To meet expectations, Germans spare no effort. Overtime and weekend work are not uncommon when it comes to completing projects on time. In working groups, you can rely on everyone doing their part.

10. SINCERITY

Reliability in Danger

Unfortunately, this virtue has lost some of its luster in recent decades. Strict adherence to deadlines is no longer a matter of course, as public projects like BER (new airport of Berlin) and Stuttgart 21 (new train station in Stuttgart) show. Berlin Brandenburg Airport, which began construction in 2006 and was supposed to be completed in 2011, did not open until 2020. A disaster that shook confidence in German punctuality. Even worse is Stuttgart 21. Construction began in 2010, and in 2024 it is still not finished. The costs have risen by 8 billion euros. Reliability is no longer the standard once expected of Germany.

This development is alarming for Germany, since its reliability has been a central value – in both private and professional life.

Despite setbacks, reliability remains a key value in German culture. It distinguishes Germans and contributes to their success. Even though projects like BER and Stuttgart 21 have damaged the image, reliability remains a strength that must be preserved.

11. PEACEFULNESS

Peacefulness means far more than just the absence of war and violence. It is a deeply rooted value in German culture, reflected in the daily lives, the interpersonal relationships, and the political attitudes of Germans.

In this chapter, we will shed light on the following aspects:

- **Listening:** The art of attentive listening as an expression of respect and appreciation.
- **Consideration:** The constant attention to the needs of others.
- **Non-violence:** The deep-rooted rejection of violence and our striving for peaceful solutions in conflict situations.
- **Pacifism:** Germany's ongoing efforts towards a more peaceful world.

11.1. Listening

In Germany, people are known for not just hearing, but truly listening. For them, listening is an expression of respect and appreciation.

The Wisdom of Silence

The German proverb "Reden ist Silber, Schweigen ist Gold" ("Speech is silver, silence is gold") emphasizes the importance of listening. Germans let others finish speaking without interruption and give them time to formulate their thoughts. Should someone interrupt nonetheless, this is immediately noticed, and a polite but firm "Please let me finish" reminds them that everyone has the right to be heard.

Active Listening: More Than Just Hearing

Germans maintain eye contact during a conversation to show interest and respect. They do not just listen passively but actively try to understand the other person.

I often missed this kind of listening abroad. For example, during my studies in the USA, I sometimes felt that while Americans heard what I was saying, they weren't really listening. It often seemed like they were just waiting to say something themselves instead of engaging with my words.

Modesty and Avoiding the Spotlight

Germans tend to be modest and reserved, often shying away from self-promotion or boasting about their accomplishments. Instead, they prioritize giving others the space to express themselves and typically focus the conversation on the other person before turning the attention to themselves. This cultural value is reflected in the German saying, "Der Esel nennt sich immer zuerst" ("The donkey always names himself first"), which is often used to admonish someone who talks about themselves too much.

Interestingly, the German language itself reinforces this cultural emphasis on modesty. While in English, the pronoun "I" is always capitalized, in German, the pronouns for "you" ("Du" and "Sie") are capitalized, while "I" ("ich") is not. This subtle difference in written form further illustrates the German cultural value of placing others before oneself.

Calmness and Empathy

Even in heated discussions, they remain calm and objective, striving to understand the other person's perspective and find solutions together. This way of listening is key to peaceful conflict resolution and helps to avoid misunderstandings and develop a better understanding of each other.

11.2. Consideration

In Germany, great importance is placed on respecting the needs and wishes of others. This consideration is evident in many small but significant gestures of everyday life.

Consideration in Everyday Life

In public spaces, Germans speak quietly so as not to disturb others. They leave common areas clean and tidy.

Men avoid "manspreading" (sitting with their legs wide open) on public transport to ensure that their fellow passengers have enough space.

They also naturally hold the door open for someone walking behind them – a simple gesture that shows they are aware of their fellow human beings.

Smoking is restricted to designated areas, and even there, they make sure that the smoke does not blow into other people's faces.

When coughing or sneezing, they use their elbow or a handkerchief to prevent the spread of germs to others.

Making Space for Others

Germans are mindful about creating space for others, whether on public transport, in queues, or at public events. They take care to avoid blocking anyone's path and expect the same courtesy in return. So, when others don't pay attention to this "unspoken rule," it can be quite irritating. For instance, it frustrates them when a group of young people strolls side-by-side, monopolizing the entire sidewalk and preventing others from passing.

In many other countries, friends walking side by side might not even notice they're obstructing anyone; it's just a relaxed way to enjoy each other's company. Yet, this casual approach can unintentionally lead to behaviors that feel inconsiderate to many Germans who value clear pathways for everyone.

Consideration on Public Transport

Public transport in Germany operates according to clear rules of consideration. When boarding crowded trains or buses, Germans queue up in an orderly fashion and let those disembarking pass first. This rule is deeply ingrained in the culture and is enforced. I often observe how people who try to board prematurely are politely but firmly reprimanded by Germans. Tourists or people from other cultures, in particular, sometimes react with surprise because they are not familiar with this unwritten rule of "let people get off first."

In summary, Germans take care throughout the day not to disturb others and to treat them with respect. In return, they expect to be treated with the same respect. This give and take creates a harmonious coexistence.

11.3. Non-Violence

In Germany, violence is considered an absolute taboo. This value is reflected in the proverb *"Der Klügere gibt nach"* ("The smarter one yields"), which reminds us that it is sometimes better to take a step back and keep a cool head instead of escalating a dispute.

Violence is an Absolute No-Go

In conflict situations, Germans maintain calm and composure and do not allow themselves to be provoked. Even if their honor is violated by verbal attacks, they do not resort to physical violence. They are aware that words can hurt, but violence is never the right answer. Physical violence or threats are completely unacceptable.

The increasing number of knife attacks, often committed by foreign offenders, worries many in Germany, who are proud that their cities have been considered safe and peaceful until now. Everything is being done to ensure that this remains the case.

Direct Communication Instead of Violence

Germans value direct and factual communication in resolving conflicts. They prefer open conversations where arguments can be exchanged and solutions found. This direct approach to conflict resolution distinguishes them from other cultures that tend to use more indirect methods or mediators.

This absolute rejection of any violence contributes to creating a peaceful and respectful society where conflicts are resolved in a civilized and non-violent manner.

11.4. Pacifism

The horrors of the two World Wars have left deep scars on the German soul. These traumatic experiences, which cost millions of people their lives and left the country in ruins, have taught a lesson that Germans will never forget: war is not a solution, but only brings suffering and destruction.

Peace as a Political Stance

Pacifism often shapes German politics through a cautious stance towards military interventions. A striking example was the 2002 federal election, when Gerhard Schröder and the SPD were significantly behind Edmund Stoiber and the CDU/CSU. But when US President George W. Bush asked for support for the invasion of Iraq, Schröder resolutely said "no," while Stoiber sided with the USA. The Germans, convinced of the rejection of an Iraq war, voted Schröder and his SPD to victory.

This pacifist attitude is also reflected in the Ukraine conflict, especially in the discussion about arms deliveries. When Chancellor Olaf Scholz hesitated to supply Taurus cruise missiles to Ukraine, he found strong support among the population.

Pacifism was also noticeable in the 2024 elections. Parties like the Alternative für Deutschland (AfD - Alternative for Germany)and Bündnis Sahra Wagenknecht (BSW), which opposed further arms deliveries, gained votes, while the Greens, who were traditionally pacifist but advocated for more arms deliveries, were punished by voters.

Pacifism: A Divide Between the Elite and the People

There is a clear difference in attitudes towards pacifism between the German elite – consisting of managers, politicians, investors, and media representatives – and the general population. The elites tend to favor military action to as they say "secure peace militarily." The majority of the population, on the other hand, takes a strictly pacifist stance and wants to avoid war at all costs, even if it supposedly prevents future conflicts.

Commitment to Peace

However, pacifism in Germany is not limited to politics. Many Germans are actively committed to peace, participating in peace demonstrations, and supporting disarmament to create a more peaceful world.

Germans are proud of their pacifist stance and continue to work towards resolving conflicts peacefully.

12. DISCIPLINE AND OBEDIENCE

Discipline and obedience – two concepts that have been closely linked to German identity for centuries and shape the idea of order and a functioning community.

But what do these values really mean to Germans? How do they manifest themselves in their everyday lives, their work ethic, and their relationship to authority?

This chapter offers fascinating insights into:
- **Following Rules:** The strong obedience of Germans.
- **Sense of Duty:** The inner compass that drives Germans to take responsibility and contribute to the common good.
- **Respect for State Authority:** A balancing act between obedience and critical thinking.
- **Cleanliness:** The German passion for cleanliness and order, especially in public spaces.
- **Tranquility:** The appreciation of silence as a sign of consideration and self-control.

12.1. Adherence to Rules

In Germany, rules are the invisible mechanism that keeps society running smoothly. Following rules is not only considered necessary for a functioning coexistence but also as an expression of respect and responsibility toward the community.

Historical Roots: The Spirit of Order

The deeply rooted adherence to rules has its origins far back in German history. Even Martin Luther, who challenged the authority of the Catholic Church in the 16th century, placed great emphasis on the rules of the Bible and stressed discipline and order in everyday life. The Protestant communities that emerged from the Reformation developed strict codes of conduct that shaped daily life, from work ethics to frugality and honesty.

The Prussian era, particularly in the 18th and 19th centuries, further reinforced these tendencies. Under kings like Frederick the Great, the so-called "Soldier King," a system of strict bureaucracy and military discipline emerged, serving as a model for other German states. Prussia's administration was legendary for its efficiency, precision, and strict adherence to rules and hierarchies. This system shaped a culture of rule-following and loyalty to the state, which still has an impact today.

The Prussian army, one of the most disciplined of its time, also served as a model for the entire society. Virtues such as obedience, punctuality, and order were highly regarded not only in the military but also in civilian life.

Discipline as a Military Success Factor

About ten years ago, during a walk in my hometown of Kyiv, I encountered soldiers from the Azov Regiment. They had recaptured a large part of the eastern Ukrainian territories from the separatists. When they learned that I was from Germany, they enthusiastically shared how they had successfully fought against separatists and Russian troops despite inferior equipment and fewer soldiers. Their secret to success, they said, lay in adhering to old German virtues: discipline, obedience, and a sense of duty.

But then came a disturbing turn. They added that Ukraine would be in a better position if the Nazi regime had won over the Soviet Union. To me, this sounded like far-right ideology, and a closer look at their flag confirmed my suspicion: it featured two Nazi symbols from the Third Reich – the Wolfsangel and the Black Sun.

It is unfortunate that German virtues such as discipline and order, which can make a nation strong, are so often associated with militarism and the Nazi regime. For these virtues are also important and valuable in a liberal and progressive society.

Rules in Everyday Life: A Dance of Discipline

Even today, adherence to rules remains deeply embedded in German culture. Traffic rules are strictly followed – even when no cars are in sight, Germans wait patiently at the red light.

Cyclists stay on the bike lanes to avoid endangering pedestrians. Following the rules is not only safer but also shows respect for others.

I vividly remember experiencing the strict adherence to rules in Germany after returning from a long stay in Asia. In Asia, it was completely normal to see an entire family – parents, three kids, and even a pet – all riding together on a single motorcycle. Everyone squeezed on somehow, even if the bike was only meant for one or two people. But when I visited my sister in Germany, things were entirely different.

My sister and brother-in-law have a family car with five seats – and, of course, five seat belts. When I suggested we take the car to go to a nearby restaurant, just 1-2 kilometers away, it was simply unthinkable for them. With their three kids, we would have been six people in a car designed for five. I offered to be the one without a seat belt, but my sister and brother-in-law looked at me in shock. They couldn't believe I was actually suggesting breaking the German law that requires everyone in the car to be buckled up at all times.

Fare evasion on public transport is seen as a breach of trust towards the system and other passengers. Germans take pride in contributing their part to ensure that public transport runs smoothly.

At checkout lines and bus stops, Germans line up neatly and wait patiently for their turn. Pushing ahead is considered extremely rude.

This is a stark contrast to other cultures. For example, just last week in Mumbai, I wanted to buy a train ticket to Ahmedabad and had to join one of three long lines. But people kept cutting in from the left and right. Each time, I would signal politely that it was my turn. Usually, I'd get a smile and a "Okay, I understand," and the person would step back – only to try cutting in again a few minutes later.

But it didn't make me angry anymore. I had learned that not every culture follows the rules as strictly as the Germans do. Instead of getting upset, I took it in stride, seeing it as part of the charm and the unique experience of being in a different country.

This adherence to rules is also evident in extraordinary situations. During the COVID-19 pandemic, Germans quickly and diligently implemented new measures such as mask mandates and contact restrictions without much fuss. This

12. DISCIPLINE AND OBEDIENCE

underscores their ability to adapt to new regulations when they serve the common good.

Guardians of Rule Compliance

Germans find it difficult to ignore rule violations, especially when it comes to traffic rules. They expect everyone to follow the rules and are often unwilling to turn a blind eye when this is not the case. This expectation of order can sometimes be met with surprise in other cultures.

A personal example of this occurred during an excursion to the Sinai Desert in Egypt. Our Bedouin driver let his ten-year-old son steer the bus while he himself calmly smoked a cigarette. Most of the fellow travelers, including many Europeans and Americans, reacted calmly, even though the boy could barely reach the gas pedal. The German travelers, on the other hand, were shocked and outraged that a child without a driver's license had taken the wheel. For them, this was an obvious rule violation that could not be tolerated. Some of them even demanded that the bus be stopped so they could switch to another vehicle.

Through their adherence to rules, Germans create a safe, orderly, and respectful society based on trust and mutual consideration.

12.2. Sense of Duty

In Germany, a sense of duty is more than just completing tasks — it is a deeply ingrained value that emphasizes responsibility, loyalty, and the common good. The proverb *"Tu deine Pflicht und vertrau auf Gott"* ("Do your duty and trust in God") aptly summarizes the German attitude: people take on their tasks with dedication and awareness of their responsibility to the community.

A Legacy of Prussian Virtues

This sense of duty has its roots in Prussian history. In the 19th century, Frederick William I, the "Soldier King" of Prussia, shaped the image of discipline and fulfillment of duty. He saw himself as a servant of his people and placed the common good above personal interests. These Prussian virtues – discipline, sense of duty, and community spirit – continue to shape German culture today.

Oaths: A Promise for Life

This sense of duty is reflected in the oaths that civil servants and soldiers take when they assume office. Civil servants swear to uphold the Constitution and fulfill their duties conscientiously, while soldiers vow to bravely defend the freedom of the Federal Republic of Germany. These oaths are not empty words but a serious promise that is fulfilled with the utmost loyalty.

Sense of Duty in the Workplace

This sense of duty is clearly evident in the German workplace. Employees are considered reliable and loyal; they take their tasks seriously and often go above and beyond to do their best work.

12. DISCIPLINE AND OBEDIENCE

Corruption: An Attack on the Common Good

An essential aspect of the German sense of duty is the resolute rejection of corruption. In Germany, political and economic decisions are expected to be made independently of personal financial interests. This principle is deeply ingrained in German culture, and deviations from it are met with widespread outrage.

However, in other countries, corruption is often perceived differently, as I myself experienced. During my stay in Delhi, India, I lived together with wealthy friends in a magnificent villa. Despite their visible wealth, my friends were very reticent about their professional activities. I often wondered how they had come to their prosperity until one day I met their business partners. They invited me to a luxurious restaurant, and there I learned the background of their business.

These partners ran a successful jewelry store that over time had become an important hub for politicians who laundered corruptions money there in the form of jewelry. Through these relationships, my acquaintances penetrated deeper and deeper into the circles of corruption, which was particularly prevalent in the upper echelons of Indian judiciary and politics.

One of their business partners proudly told me about a current case in which one of the richest families in India was trying to obtain a large compensation payment of more than a billion USD for land that had been expropriated from them by the state decades ago. A judge of the highest courts in an Indian state had contacted my acquaintances and offered to rule in favor of this family – but on the condition that he received a significant portion of the compensation as a commission. For my acquaintances, this was a common deal that gave them the possibility to earn many millions USD.

However, the reason they invited me was even more interesting. They had contacts with high-ranking politicians who had lucrative contracts to award in the field of renewable energy. My role in this network was to negotiate contracts with German companies that could supply these renewable energy solutions as an intermediary, collect a commission, and pass it on to the politicians involved. It would have been an easy way to make a lot of money, and the deal seemed perfectly prepared. Nevertheless, I could not bring myself to go down this path. My German sense of duty and my abhorrence of corruption kept me from participating in such a scheme.

I had similar experiences during the COVID-19 pandemic when I procured FFP2 masks through my contacts in China and sold them in Latin America. Numerous middlemen demanded high bribes, which drove up the prices of urgently needed masks. Corruption was so normalized there that there was an unofficial rule: a maximum of 40% of the purchase price could be used for bribes and in return the police would not get involved. This practice was so established that it almost seemed like a legitimate part of the business. Such experiences opened my eyes to the extent of corruption in many parts of the world, where the sense of duty that exists in Germany seems to play hardly any role.

In Germany, however, even the mere appearance of corruption causes a scandal. A striking example is the case of former Federal President Christian Wulff, who came under fire for a private loan that he received from a befriended businessman. Although there was no public damage and the loan was duly repaid, his political career ended abruptly. The outrage was great because in Germany, corruption is understood as a direct attack on the common good.

12. DISCIPLINE AND OBEDIENCE

However, behind this facade of incorruptibility lies a different reality as I have found out myself. In recent years, corruption in Germany—particularly among the elites in business, politics, and media—has increased. Numerous scandals surrounding the procurement of protective masks and other medical supplies during the Corona pandemic illustrate this vividly.

During the Corona pandemic I spoke with many German colleagues who facilitated the procurement of FFP2 masks—not in Latin America, as I did, but in Germany. While I thought that 40% in kickbacks was significant, they reported entirely different scenarios. They emphasized that in Germany, it's impossible to win a public tender without connections to high-ranking politicians. Furthermore, the prices paid by the German government were often more than double the usual market prices. Millions of taxpayer euros were wasted, while significant sums flowed back to intermediaries and politicians through commission payments.

Notable examples include Andrea Tandler, the daughter of former Bavarian state minister Georg Tandler, who earned over 48 million euros in commissions within only 6 weeks, and CSU (Bavarian part of the German conservative party CDU) politicians Alfred Sauter and Georg Nüßlein, who also became millionaires through mask procurement.

These examples underscore that corruption is a lucrative business in Germany, primarily benefiting the elite. While the general population has a strong sense of justice and a clear rejection of corruption, the moral fabric in the upper echelons appears to be crumbling.

Nonetheless, the "ordinary citizens" still maintain a strong sense of rule of law and an absolute rejection of corruption. This leads to continued trust in German institutions.

12.3. Respect for Authority

Respect for authority is deeply rooted in Germany, like the roots of an old oak tree firmly anchored in the ground. This respect is evident in interactions with the police, military, administration, and even teachers.

Historical Roots

This respect goes back to Prussian history, where obedience and discipline were considered cornerstones of the state under Frederick William I, the "Soldier King." These virtues contributed significantly to Prussia's success and stability.

However, National Socialism took this respect in a dangerous direction: it was perverted and abused into blind obedience to the regime, leading to crimes of unimaginable proportions.

This showed the negative aspect of blind respect for authority. Imagine Nazi leaders like Hitler, Goering, or Himmler having to shoot peaceful, law-abiding citizens because they were Jewish or, even worse, filling gas chambers with poisonous gas. Most likely, their consciences would not have allowed them to execute their own orders. Instead, others, low in the hierarchy executed on the order. These people who had to do the "dirty" work, and probably knew that what they were doing was wrong, followed orders blindly because, to them, any order had to be followed.

This bitter lesson of what the blind following of orders can lead to has led Germans, after 1945, to question and critically examine unreflective respect for authority.

12. DISCIPLINE AND OBEDIENCE

Two Camps in Dealing with State Authority

Today, two different perspectives on respect for state authority exist in Germany: the socialist-progressives and the liberal-conversatives.

The Socialist-Progressive Camp

This group, often voters of parties like the SPD, the Greens, or the Left. This camp is most closely aligned with the Democratic party in the USA. They call for a strong state with comprehensive social services. However, they also criticize institutions such as the police and the military sharply. While they have great respect for political decision-makers and those in administration who manage financial resources and make decisions, they have little trust in the executive officials enforcing the law, such as the police and the military.

The Liberal-Conservative Camp

Supporters of the CDU, FDP, and AfD (the German parties that want more freedom for the population and support conservative values) advocate for a leaner state with less intervention. This camp is most closely aligned with the traditional Republican party (CDU, FDP) and in particular the MAGA movement of Donald Trump (AfD) in the USA. They prefer to give politicians and administrative personnel less power and funding. On the other hand, they show great respect for the police and military, viewing these institutions as guarantors of security and order, and they appreciate their contribution to social cohesion.

The majority of Germans lean toward the liberal-conservative camp and view increasing state spending critically, fearing it might stifle creativity and innovation. At the same time, they acknowledge the necessity of state structures and trust that civil servants will carry out their duties responsibly. For this reason, they have a high respect for the police and military.

This ambivalent relationship with state authority became particularly evident during the Corona pandemic. Many liberal-conservative citizens criticized the government measures, but respect for the police who enforced these measures largely remained. Criticism was directed more at political decision-makers than at the police themselves.

Respect in Everyday Life: A Core Value in Various Areas

Despite the critical engagement with authority, respect for state institutions remains a central value in Germany. This respect is evident in many areas of daily life:

Respect for the Police

The police stand for safety and order. They are treated with courtesy, their instructions are followed, and people support them in their work. Even when their actions are questioned, this is done respectfully.

Respect for Civil Servants and Public Service

Civil servants and public service employees are treated with appreciation because they perform important tasks for society. Whether in administration or healthcare, people appreciate their efforts and are cooperative in dealing with them.

Respect for Teachers

Teachers are also held in high regard, as they not only impart knowledge but also serve as role models for the next generation. They accompany students on their educational journey, shaping their values and skills.

However, many teachers report that this respect has steadily declined in recent years. Disrespectful behavior from both students and parents has become more common, making it harder to maintain a relationship of mutual trust.

Respect on Public Transport

This respect is also evident on public transport. Train staff and conductors are treated politely, tickets are readily shown, and people express gratitude for their service, which contributes to a smooth process.

Respect for the Military

Soldiers who defend the country enjoy great respect in Germany. Their commitment is valued, and people treat them with gratitude for their service.

Respect for state authority remains an integral part of German culture, even though it is now accompanied by critical awareness. It is a respect based on recognition and understanding – not on blind obedience.

12.4. Cleanliness

For Germans, cleanliness is an expression of respect, discipline, and community spirit, deeply rooted in their value culture.

They believe that a clean environment not only pleases the eye, but also enhances well-being, conveys a sense of order and security, and ultimately contributes to a more harmonious coexistence.

Public Space: Their Shared Living Room

Cleanliness in public spaces is particularly important to Germans. They consider it an extension of their own four walls, a shared living room that they all share and want to feel comfortable in. Therefore, they are often even more meticulous in keeping public spaces spotless than their own homes.

Littering: A Matter of Honor and Decency

In Germany, carelessly throwing away trash is an absolute no-go, an act of inconsideration. Germans use the designated trash cans with a naturalness that almost borders on ritual. And if there isn't one in sight? Then they patiently carry their trash around with them as if it were a precious commodity until they find one – even if that means lugging it all the way home.

Some of them even go a step further and collect other people's trash while walking in nature. In almost all communities, there are so-called Cleanup Days where volunteers pick up trash from the streets in their free time. These quiet heroes of everyday life ensure that their surroundings remain clean.

Toilet Hygiene

For Germans, it's especially important to leave the toilet clean after use. That's why many men prefer to sit down when urinating, to avoid unpleasant splashes that might bother the next user. I still vividly remember how my mother used to remind me as a child to always sit down. At home, it was a strict rule, and even in public restrooms, she taught me the German hygiene principle: If you pee standing up, always wipe the toilet rim thoroughly afterwards.

In Germany, it is unthinkable to relieve oneself in public. Such behavior is considered extremely unhygienic and inconsiderate. Of course, it can happen that someone urgently needs to go and there is no toilet nearby. In this case, Germans discreetly look for a secluded spot in the forest or park, but they would never pee or shit in a public squares or streets.

Their beloved pets should not cause uncleanliness either. When walking their dogs, they always carry dog waste bags and properly dispose of their four-legged friends' droppings. It is a sign of respect for their fellow human beings. After all, nobody wants to step in dog poop.

Cleanliness in Public Spaces

Germans leave restaurants and supermarkets the way they would like to find them: clean and tidy. In fast food restaurants, they clear their trays and wipe the table. They also return used shopping carts to the designated area so that they do not get in the way of other customers.

They are also careful not to leave any trash on public transport. And they leave their feet on the floor, not on the seats. After all, they don't want to sit on dirty seats or ride in a dirty train themselves.

When Germans visit someone, they are especially careful not to bring in any dirt. Therefore, it is customary, especially in East Germany, to take off your shoes at the entrance.

Changing Times: The Challenge of the "Broken Window Theory"

Unfortunately, there is a worrying change in terms of cleanliness and littering. The once sparkling clean German trains are increasingly looking dirty. Trash lies carelessly on the seats or in the aisle, and young people seem to prefer placing their shoes on the seats rather than on the floor.

Also, at McDonald's and other fast-food chains, fewer and fewer people are seen clearing their trays after they have finished eating. It seems as if respect for public space is dwindling among some people.

I particularly notice the littering in the morning when I go for a run. Almost every day I have to pick up trash that people have simply left on or in front of our property.

This indicates a decline in values with regard to cleanliness in public spaces. It may be that the people who throw their trash in our hedge would not do so in their own homes. And maybe they continue to take their own hygiene seriously. But unfortunately, there are more and more people who seem to be indifferent to public space. They think that "the public" will take care of it.

This problem is exacerbated by the "Broken Window Theory." The theory states that even small signs of neglect, such as a broken window or litter lying around, can trigger a chain reaction that leads to crime and social decay.

The broken window that no one repairs, or even litter lying around, sends the message: "Nobody cares here, rules don't apply." This encourages further violations of rules, and the sense of order and security erodes. The neighborhood

12. DISCIPLINE AND OBEDIENCE

deteriorates, and a breeding ground for bigger problems is created.

The Broken Window Theory shows how important it is to pay attention to even small signs of disorder and to take countermeasures early on.

Glimmer of Hope: The Younger Generation

For this reason, I personally make an effort to collect the trash around our property almost every day to maintain order and cleanliness and prevent crime and social problems. And there is hope! Recently, as I was collecting trash, a boy stopped with his scooter to help me. He said that too many people just throw their trash on the street, and he thought it was great that I was cleaning up – he wanted to help me!

This showed me that even in the younger generation, there are still people who care about the value of cleanliness in public spaces.

Cleanliness is and remains a central value in German culture, especially when it comes to public space. It is a value that must be preserved and passed on to future generations so that Germany remains a country where people feel comfortable and safe.

12.5. Tranquility

In Germany, tranquility is more than just the absence of noise – it is a central component of discipline and respect for others. This appreciation for quietude permeates many aspects of daily life and allows Germans to focus on what is important without being distracted by unnecessary sounds.

Public Spaces: Oases of Calm

The deep connection to tranquility is particularly evident in public areas. Libraries, doctor's offices, and public transport become oases of silence where conversations are held only in whispers. Loud phone calls or music are frowned upon, and excessively loud behavior is often met with frowns and disapproving glances.

Tranquility at a Young Age

The cultivation of this culture of tranquility begins in childhood. Parents teach their children early on that boisterous romping or loud screaming in public is not acceptable. Instead, they learn to control their volume and be considerate of their surroundings. This lesson in self-control and social responsibility accompanies them throughout their lives.

Quiet Hours: A Sacred Principle

Quiet hours are firmly established in Germany and are a sign of the desire for harmonious coexistence. In residential areas, there are strict quiet hours during which noise-intensive activities such as mowing the lawn or playing loud music are prohibited. These rules are particularly sacred on Sundays and public holidays.

I remember visiting my father in Germany, wanting to do something nice for him. The grass in the garden was overgrown, and I thought it would be a good idea to mow it. I had barely started when my father suddenly came rushing out into the garden, frantically waving his arms for me to stop immediately. "Why?" I asked, surprised. "The lawn is long overdue for a trim!" But my father looked at me, horrified, and

12. DISCIPLINE AND OBEDIENCE

exclaimed: "Eike, it's Sunday! We can't make that kind of noise today!" At that moment, I realized I had committed a cardinal sin in Germany: I tried to mow the lawn on a Sunday!

Tranquility in All Areas of Life

Tranquility is an important factor not only in private but also in professional life. In offices, especially open-plan offices, there are often special quiet zones where concentrated work is possible. Loud conversations or phone calls are held in designated areas so as not to disturb colleagues. Restaurants and cafés are also places of relaxation. Loud conversations or music that disturb the shared meal are considered impolite.

Recently, I was at Burger King and took a business video call. After a few minutes, a gentleman came over and asked me to end my conversation because I was in a restaurant and not in my office. I found this to be very exaggerated – after all, we were at Burger King and not in a fine dining establishment. But I had to give in to the German addiction to peace and quiet.

Even reading or reading aloud in public is perceived as disturbing. Quiet behavior is an expression of mindfulness and respect for the needs of others. I remember a few years ago when I wanted to brush up on my Chinese and while riding on the train was quietly reading the Chinese text to myself. Although this was very quiet, just mumbling, it wasn't long before other passengers asked me to just stay completely quiet.

Cultural Differences: When Loudness Meets Silence

The German penchant for tranquility becomes particularly noticeable when different cultures meet. What is considered normal in some countries – loud conversations in the supermarket or shouting on the street – can quickly be perceived as disruptive and disrespectful in Germany. This cultural difference can lead to misunderstandings.

I remember staying in a hotel in South Asia. It was 4 a.m., and I had just fallen asleep when I was suddenly woken up by a loud noise: **BUM – BUM – BUM**. Then it went silent. I closed my eyes again, only to be startled awake a few minutes later: **Bum – bum – bum**. Half asleep, I hesitated for a moment, then threw on some clothes and stepped out of my room, curious to see what was going on.

Right outside my door, a few workers were busy repairing a filtration system, making an incredible racket in the middle of the night. When they saw me, they just gave me a big smile and cheerfully called out, "Hello, Sir!" No trace of embarrassment, no apology – they were simply in a good mood, as if this were the most normal thing in the world. I paused for a second, smiled back, and calmly asked if it might be possible to continue the work a bit later. They nodded cheerfully and carried on as if nothing had happened.

In Germany, I probably would have reacted very differently, full of indignation, convinced that my right to peace and quiet had been violated. But in that moment, I realized I was in a completely different culture, where noise and chaos are perceived differently – simply more relaxed.

You can notice this difference, too, when children from foreign families play louder than is typical in Germany. German parents tend to intervene quickly, asking their kids to be quiet. In the native culture of the foreigners, however, lively play is no cause for concern, even when it gets noisy. So the parents will not intervene, which Germans might perceive as disrespectful.

12. DISCIPLINE AND OBEDIENCE

Germans strive to create a quiet and pleasant environment through their behavior. By respecting tranquility, they show consideration and respect for the community and their fellow human beings.

13. ACCURACY

From immaculately organized factory floors to masterpieces of precision engineering – the German passion for accuracy is omnipresent. It is more than just a quality feature; it is an attitude towards life that is reflected in punctuality, diligence, and orderliness.

This chapter delves into the world of German accuracy and explores how this value shapes everyday life, work, and social interaction:

- **Punctuality:** The German appreciation for punctuality as an expression of respect and professionalism.
- **Diligence:** Paying attention to every detail to achieve perfect quality.
- **Orderliness:** The importance of order and structure for efficiency, reliability, and harmonious coexistence.

13.1. Punctuality

In Germany, punctuality is more than just a virtue – it is an expression of respect and professionalism. Time is seen as a precious commodity, and therefore great importance is placed on not wasting it, neither for oneself nor for others. The German proverb *"Pünktlichkeit ist die Höflichkeit der Könige"* ("Punctuality is the courtesy of kings") sums this up perfectly: being on time means valuing the other person's time.

Adherence to Appointments

Whether it's a business meeting, a date, or a doctor's appointment – being on time is a matter of course in Germany.

People arrive punctually, often even a few minutes early, to be ready as soon as the meeting officially begins.

World Champion in Punctuality

When I lived in Barcelona, I organized a party and invited friends of different nationalities. The Germans? They were, of course, on time. The French and Americans arrived with a charming little delay, which didn't surprise me. But the Spaniards? They didn't call until 30 minutes after the agreed time to say they would be even later. When they finally arrived, I thought they would apologize. But they just smiled relaxedly, as if it were completely normal. At that moment I realized: In Spain, being late in a private setting is not a cause for concern, but almost part of the experience.

Another time I was invited to a party hosted by Spaniards. With my Spanish companion, I stood punctually at the door, ready to ring the bell. But suddenly she held me back and said we should wait a little longer. It turned out that in Spain it is considered more polite not to arrive exactly at the agreed time to give the hosts time to prepare. For someone like me, who understands punctuality as respect, that was hard to grasp. But it showed me that the handling of time differs from culture to culture.

Even artificial intelligence recognizes these differences. We asked an AI how much delay is acceptable for an invitation in various countries. The AI presented us with the following chart:

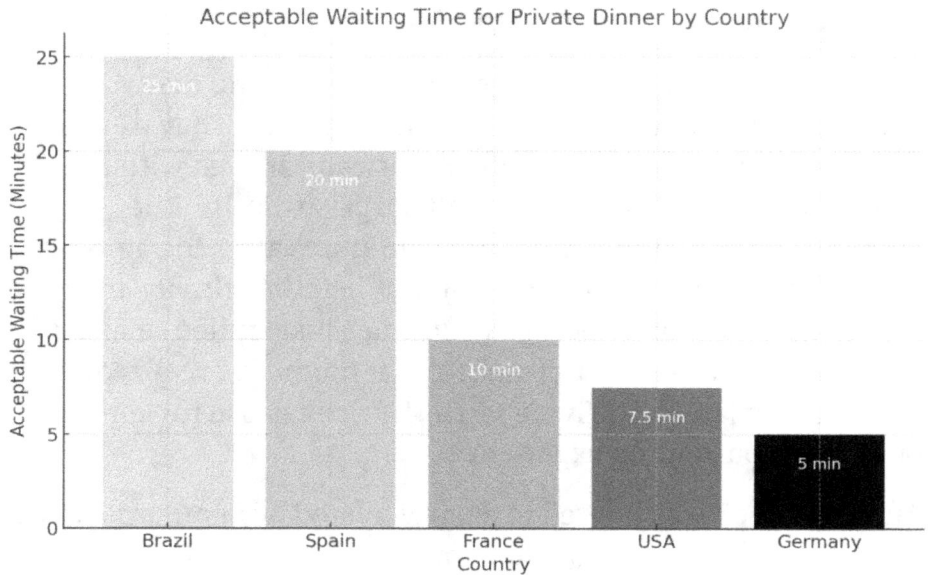

Time Management

The reason for punctuality in Germany lies in effective time management. The day is carefully planned, and potential delays due to traffic or unforeseen events are taken into account. This planning ensures that there is always enough buffer time to arrive on time.

During my stays abroad, however, I noticed that this aspiration is not shared equally everywhere. Often, when I asked "How long will it take?" I would get vague answers like "Not long." I found such vagueness frustrating and would ask: "Exactly how many minutes?" In response, I often only heard "Just a few minutes." When I asked again: "Okay, but exactly how many minutes?", I usually only received annoyed looks. After several such situations, I realized that few cultures have a similar relationship with punctuality as Germany.

When Something Comes Up...

Germans find being late extremely unpleasant. Should it happen nevertheless, those affected apologize profusely. However, spontaneous cancellations or last-minute changes are difficult to accept – it is expected that such changes are communicated in advance.

"Punctual like Deutsche Bahn"

However, the attitude towards punctuality is changing. The expression *"Pünktlich wie die Deutsche Bahn"* ("Punctual like Deutsche Bahn") used to be genuine praise and stood for the proverbial reliability of Deutsche Bahn (German Railways). Back then, you could rely on trains running on time. Today, however, this saying has been reversed – it is often used ironically, as delays on the railway have almost become the norm. This change reflects a generally greater tolerance for unpunctuality, which is increasingly observed among many Germans themselves.

Despite this, punctuality remains a central value in German culture. It is still valued as a sign of respect and professionalism and remains part of the cultural identity, even in a changing world.

13.2. Perfectionism

Perfectionism is firmly embedded in the cultural DNA of Germans, almost like a genetic code that shapes their daily lives, their work, and their self-perception. These values form the foundation of the precision and quality that they expect and value in everything they do.

A Polish Craftsman in Germany

A Polish craftsman I once met told me a story that perfectly illustrated the difference between his homeland and Germany. In Poland, he said, improvisation and creative problem-solving are often required. In Germany, on the other hand, even the smallest details are scrutinized, and any deviation from the plan is closely questioned. His anecdote was humorous, but it contained a kernel of truth: the German dedication to accuracy is deeply rooted and sometimes difficult for outsiders to comprehend.

"Made in Germany": A Worldwide Seal of Quality

This appreciation for German precision and quality is also encountered abroad. During my stay in Egypt, my landlord proudly pointed out that my apartment had been built by a German. He assured me that this meant it met quality standards that no other apartment in Egypt could achieve. It was a nice example of how the "Made in Germany" label stands for durability and reliability worldwide – a symbol of the care and accuracy that goes into German products.

For Germans, it is often not about producing things quickly and cheaply, but about creating a truly good product that meets the highest standards and of which they can be proud. Even the smallest flaws, which the customer might never notice, can keep craftsmen and engineers awake at night.

13. ACCURACY

This attention to detail is also reflected in everyday life. Daily tasks such as cooking, repairing a bicycle, or filling out forms are carried out carefully and accurately to avoid mistakes and achieve the best possible result.

Perfectionism: Both a Curse and a Blessing

But perfectionism can also be a hindrance. Sometimes it stands in the way and prevents progress from being made. In business, it can often be better to bring a product to market quickly rather than spending too long fine-tuning it to perfection and missing valuable time and opportunities.

The high standards of diligence sometimes lead to Germans being perceived as fussy or overly critical. Because perfection is expected, they quickly notice and criticize mistakes and imperfections. In international work environments, this direct approach can be perceived as overly critical or impolite.

Despite these challenges, diligence and accuracy remain central values that shape Germany.

13.3. Orderliness

"Ordnung ist das halbe Leben" ("Orderliness is half of life") – this proverb is more than just an empty phrase in Germany; it's a philosophy of life. It reflects the belief that a structured and organized life is the key to efficiency, satisfaction, and inner peace.

Order vs. Cleanliness: Two Sides of the Same Coin

Order and cleanliness are closely intertwined, but they are not the same thing. Cleanliness refers to purity and hygiene, while order is a principle of structuring and systematization. In Germany, order occupies a special place: everything has its fixed place, processes are clearly defined, and chaos finds no room. This importance of order has been captured by the following meme that is entitled:

Chaos according to Germans

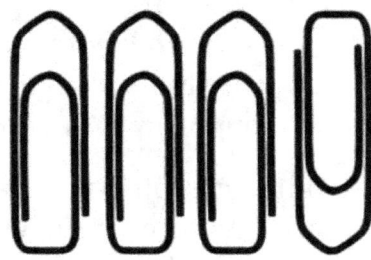

Order from an Early Age

This love of order is taught in childhood. *"Räum deine Spielsachen weg!"* ("Put your toys away!") — a sentence that is probably heard in every German child's room. While in other cultures the playful chaos of childhood is often tolerated, German parents emphasize structure and order, even in the children's room. This is how children learn the importance of organization early on.

Order at Work

Many Germans prefer a tidy, almost empty desk. A clear desk seems to promote a clear mind, free from distractions. Every object has its designated place and is put back after use.

13. ACCURACY

Even in the digital world, many Germans maintain structure. Files are carefully organized in folders, emails are systematically archived, and appointments are precisely entered in calendars – whether analog or digital. This order helps to maintain an overview and avoid data chaos.

Personally, I have observed this German love of order especially in software development. German developers attach great importance to clean and orderly code structures. I often heard them criticize when other developers opted for quick solutions rather than high-quality code. Developers from other cultures often asked: "My code works, why does it have to be tidier?" This attitude met with incomprehension from German developers. Many software entrepreneurs therefore prefer to work with German developers because they know that the long-term quality and maintainability of the code is better.

Even if not every German is an order fanatic, the love of order is deeply rooted in the culture. It shapes thinking and action in many areas, promotes efficiency and reliability, and is an essential part of the German success culture.

14. WORK ETHIC

From tireless diligence to a results-oriented mindset – work ethic is a fundamental principle of German values and forms the foundation for both personal and collective success.

In the following sections, we explore the core values that define this work ethic and how they are expressed in various areas of life:

- **Diligence:** The tireless effort and commitment that not only form the basis for personal success but also represent the engine of Germany's economic progress.
- **Speed:** From the quick processing of everyday tasks to the rapid pace on the Autobahn.
- **Productivity:** It's about achieving the best results in the shortest possible time.
- **Achievement Orientation:** It is the belief that honest work, discipline, and dedication are the path to success.

14.1. Diligence

Germans are known for their hard work. The German proverb *"Ohne Fleiß, kein Preis"* ("No pain, no gain" or more literally "no hard work, no prize") is firmly anchored in German culture and shapes their thinking and actions.

Diligence as an Engine of Success

The willingness to work hard and continuously is not only a prerequisite for one's own success but also the driving force behind Germany's economic advancement. Even abroad, Germans are considered diligent and reliable workers. Another proverb that reflects this attitude well is *"Disziplin ist der Schlüssel zum Erfolg"* ("Discipline is the key to success"). This discipline and perseverance shape their actions, both professionally and privately. Even when obstacles or distractions arise, they consistently pursue their goals.

The Roots of the German Work Ethic

Hard work is considered one of the highest virtues in Germany. From an early age, children are taught in school that hard work and continuous effort lead to good results. This attitude accompanies Germans into their professional lives, where they are expected to carry out tasks with great commitment and perseverance. Success is rarely left to chance but is seen as the result of hard work and perseverance. Similar to ants, many Germans work diligently and save a lot. This mentality has made Germany one of the leading economic nations.

Changing Times

However, a shift has taken place in recent decades. The strong work ethic that prevailed until the 1980s has lost intensity. The introduction of the 40-hour week and the desire for a better work-life balance have led to many employees working less. Well-paid employees today often consciously choose to work less to have more time for family, hobbies, and personal interests.

For these reasons, the average annual working time has fallen sharply and, in international comparison, is far behind many other countries, as can be seen in the graph below.

THE GERMAN SUCCESS CULTURE

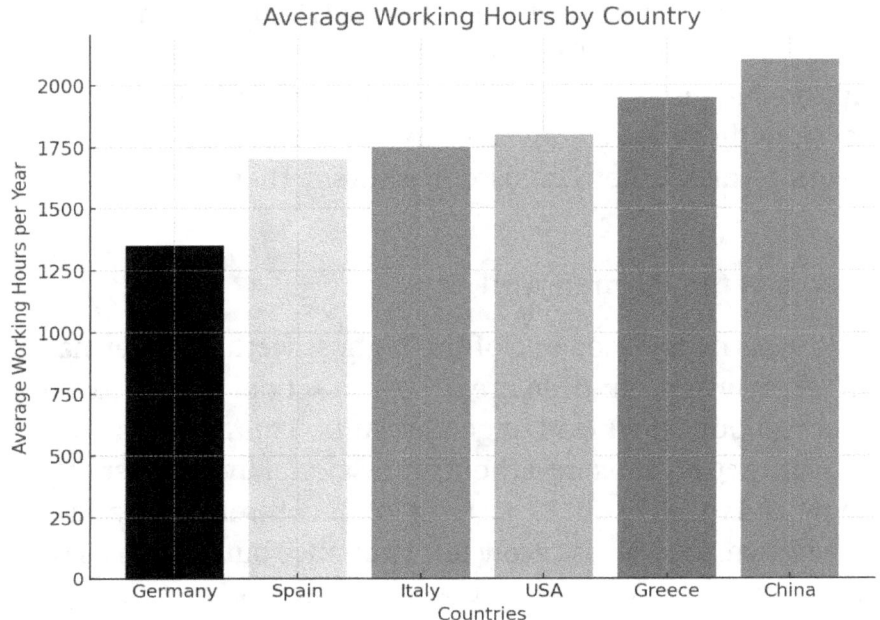

The generous sick leave policy of many German doctors has also contributed to this change. Employees are often signed off sick even with minor ailments, which leads to more days off and can give the impression that work ethic is declining.

Despite these changes, I have often found in my international work that Germans are still among the most diligent workers and are willing to make great personal sacrifices to lead the team to success. This includes working overtime, working on weekends, or stepping in for colleagues at short notice.

Despite the changes, hard work remains a central value in Germany. Many are proud of their work and strive to always give their best. Even though the world of work has changed and work-life balance has become more important, diligence remains an integral part of German identity and success.

14.2. Speed

Germans are known for getting things done quickly and efficiently, as if driven by an invisible turbocharger to avoid wasting time – especially when others are affected. Time is seen as precious, almost like a valuable drop that should be savored carefully and never wasted.

Speeding Through Life

This principle is already evident in the way they walk. While in other countries a leisurely stroll is associated with ambling and window-shopping, Germans walk briskly and purposefully. A Chinese friend once jokingly remarked that Germans tend to march when they walk – so determined and fast is their pace.

Autobahn Ballet

Nowhere is this "speed" mentality more evident than on the Autobahn. It's not just about driving fast, but also maintaining a certain minimum speed and staying as far to the right as possible. The rearview mirror is keenly observed, and lanes are changed at lightning speed when a faster vehicle approaches. This consideration is a matter of course and an expression of respect for other people's time.

Everyday Efficiency: Every Second Counts

This striving for efficiency is also evident in everyday life. At traffic lights, people start moving immediately when the light turns green. At the supermarket checkout, the money or card is already at the ready to clear the checkout area quickly. Even in public restrooms, especially on trains, care is taken to be quick, as others may be waiting urgently.

Procrastination: The Silent Saboteur

Procrastination is seen as an opponent to be defeated. Instead of postponing tasks, they are done immediately, because unused time means lost opportunities. The proverb *"Was du heute kannst besorgen, das verschiebe nicht auf morgen"* ("What you can do today, don't put off until tomorrow") shapes this behavior. It's about taking responsibility and avoiding unnecessary stress. Why burden tomorrow when it can be done today?

Speed as an Expression of Respect

Speed is more than just a behavior — it is understood as an expression of respect for other people's time. Efficient action not only brings personal benefits but also benefits the community by making meaningful use of time as a valuable resource without wasting it.

In German culture, speed and efficiency are deeply rooted in all areas of life and shape everyday actions.

14.3. Productivity

Germans are known for their strong sense of productivity. Time is seen as a precious commodity that should be used efficiently. Instead of investing more time in work, they strive to achieve the maximum in minimal time. The focus is on goal-oriented and efficient action. It's not about working longer, but smarter — "working smart" instead of only "working hard."

14. WORK ETHIC

The German Hero in the Office

A Polish colleague who has worked in both Germany and the USA described the difference aptly: "In the USA, you're the hero if you're the first to arrive and the last to leave, even working on weekends. In Germany, you're the hero if you manage to do all your work so productively that you can finish on time." This pragmatism shows that efficiency is valued more highly than the mere length of working hours.

Productivity Through Efficient Methods

In Germany, productivity is determined by smart planning and efficient working methods. The focus is on quality over quantity, and importance is placed on planning tasks in advance. Detailed to-do lists, clear priorities, and a well-thought-out structure for the workday help to avoid unnecessary interruptions.

Focus and Technology

Distraction is minimized during working hours. Social media or long private conversations take a back seat. Modern technologies such as project management tools and automation software are used to facilitate and accelerate work. Instead of being satisfied with the status quo, they are constantly looking for ways to optimize processes and increase productivity.

Productivity as a Driver for Success and Work-Life Balance

This productivity is not only part of German work culture but also an important factor in the country's economic success. It enables the development of high-quality products and services, remaining competitive, and securing jobs in the long term.

At the same time, this productivity ensures a balanced work-life balance. By completing work in the allotted time, there is room for family, friends, and leisure. This is how professional success is reconciled with a fulfilling private life.

14.4. Pursuit of Achievement

The pursuit of achievement in Germany is more than just an awareness of good work; it is an attitude towards life that permeates all areas of German life. For Germans, the pursuit of achievement is deeply rooted in their culture and shapes both everyday life and professional life. This pursuit is based on three inextricably linked principles:

- **"Leistungsbereitschaft"** (willingness to perform) = the will to achieve, motivation to perform
- **"Leistungsbewusstsein"** (achievement awareness) = understanding and awareness of the importance and value of performance
- **"Leistungsprinzip"** (merit principle) = evaluation and reward based on performance

Willingness to Perform

"Die Ärmel hochkrempeln" ("Rolling up one's sleeves") is not an empty phrase in Germany, but a lived reality. Germans are known for not only working hard but also committing themselves fully to their goals. This willingness to perform goes beyond individual success – it also encompasses the well-being of the community. This attitude is deeply ingrained in the

14. WORK ETHIC

culture, as highlighted in the 10 guidelines on German culture by Thomas de Maizière: every individual in Germany is called upon to make their contribution, be it at work or in everyday life.

Achievement Awareness: Quality and Excellence as a Standard

Germans value quality and excellence in everything they do. This achievement awareness is not only evident in their own work but also in the recognition of the achievements of others. In Germany, it is an honor to be a master of one's trade, and this status is viewed with pride and respect. This love of precision and perfection drives Germans to always give their best and ensure high quality in all areas.

Merit Principle: The Honest Path to Success

For Germans, the merit principle is a central component of their work ethic. It means that success is based on hard work, skill, and commitment – without shortcuts or tricks. The merit principle ensures that career advancement in Germany is based on performance. Hard work is valued and rewarded in German culture, and there is a belief that anyone can achieve their goals through effort and dedication.

Achievement as a Benchmark: A Life Path Shaped by Achievement

The merit principle accompanies Germans from an early age. Performance already plays a crucial role in the school system. Children in Germany are divided into different types of schools based on their academic performance, such as Hauptschule (for low achievers), Realschule, and Gymnasium (for top academic performers). This division has far-reaching implications for educational and career opportunities. The Gymnasium prepares students for university studies, while the other types of schools focus on practical vocational fields.

The merit principle remains omnipresent in university studies in Germany. Access to sought-after courses of study such as medicine or psychology is strictly regulated and depends on the school grades – a system that ensures that only the best students gain access to these subjects. This performance pressure continues in central examinations such as the law or medical examinations, that are organized on a state level and are considered to be particularly demanding.

I personally went through the grueling state exams for law, and I still remember that intense week filled with multiple exams, both written and oral, each lasting a full five hours. Compared to this, the U.S. bar exam seems almost like a walk in the park.

The merit principle is also deeply rooted in professional life. German employers pay close attention to good grades, professional qualifications, and relevant experience. Regular performance reviews and target agreements ensure that employees in Germany continuously give their best and develop further. Promotions and salary increases are generally based on demonstrable achievements.

The merit principle is also firmly established in the German civil service. Applicants undergo rigorous selection procedures in which professional skills and personal suitability are tested. Promotions and transfers are also based on performance and experience.

14. WORK ETHIC

Merit Principle Under Criticism

The merit principle is based on the assumption that performance is objectively measurable and comparable. This is the only way that positions and resources can be allocated according to performance, whether at school, at work, or in sports. However, this measurability and the associated competition are increasingly being criticized in Germany.

One example of this development are the rule changes in the Bundesjugendspiele (National Sport Games), a national sport competition across schools in the whole country. Traditionally, they served as a performance comparison in which students were measured in various sport disciplines and the best received medals or certificates of their achievements. Recently, however, there have been efforts to shift the focus away from performance measurement and towards the joy of movement and shared experience. Scoring, medals and certificates are abolished, and every participant receives a medal of participation.

Critics see this as a departure from the merit principle and pursuit of achievement, while proponents emphasize that the joy of movement and the inclusion of all students are more important than the pure performance comparison.

School Grades: Controversy Over Performance Evaluation

Similarly, the discussion around school grades highlights a shift away from the merit principle and the pursuit of achievement. School grades are meant to objectively assess students' performance, guide their educational paths, and provide an incentive to study for good results. However, in Germany, too, there are critics who argue that grades create performance pressure and fear of failure, leading some to advocate for their abolition.

So, there are also Germans who are critical of the merit principle. But still, the merit principle is often seen in Germany as a guarantor of equal opportunities. Everyone, regardless of their social background, has the opportunity to prove themselves through their performance.

However, critics argue that children from educationally disadvantaged families do not start on equal footing with those from more affluent backgrounds. They therefore advocate for fairer solutions, such as abolishing grades or awarding extra points to students from disadvantaged backgrounds to level the playing field.

Merit Principle and DEI: A Balancing Act

The push from the United States to promote DEI (Diversity, Equity, and Inclusion) is sparking a lively debate in Germany. DEI initiatives aim to dismantle structural barriers and foster equal opportunities, but many Germans see a possible clash with the meritocratic values that have long been a foundation in German society. In Germany, there's a strong belief that factors like gender, origin, or race should play no role in determining one's career or educational opportunities. To many, this means recruitment and admissions processes should be "color-blind," assessing individuals purely on their qualifications and abilities, without preference for any particular group.

The concern among many Germans is that DEI initiatives, by focusing on attributes as gender, origin, or ethnicity would mean a departure from the merit principle, which is based on the idea that success and advancement should be based solely on demonstrable skills and achievements.

Attacking the Merit Principle from Above

Interestingly, the attack on the merit principle often comes from the political elite. Politicians, who have often risen through relationships and networks, see the merit principle as a threat to their own position. They fear that a stronger focus on performance could expose their own shortcomings and therefore advocate for a weakening of the merit principle.

In contrast to the political elite, the ordinary citizen in Germany adheres firmly to the merit principle. For many Germans, it stands as a symbol of fairness and equal opportunities. They believe that hard work should be rewarded and that career advancement must be based on performance – not on relationships or privileges. Outside of politics, the awareness of achievement still remains strongly rooted in German society.

15. KNOWLEDGE SOCIETY

From the appreciation of education to the power of innovation – the concept of the knowledge society is a cornerstone of German culture. Since its foundation, Germany has established itself as a society in which rational thinking and scientific research are paramount. This tradition dates back to the 18th century, the Age of Enlightenment, and has shaped a culture that counts education and progress among its highest values.

In the following sections, we explore the core values that define this knowledge society:

- **Education**: In Germany, education is considered the key to personal development and social participation.
- **Critical Thinking**: The ability to question information in order to make informed decisions.
- **Innovation**: The innovative strength is evident in the large number of Nobel Prize winners and globally renowned research institutions.

15.1. Education

For Germans, education is invaluable and firmly anchored in their cultural DNA. Thomas de Maizière summed this up succinctly in his "10 Commandments of German guiding culture": a willingness to learn is a fundamental expectation of everyone living in Germany.

Education as a Key to Personal and Social Mobility

In Germany, education opens doors – it is the key to personal success, social participation, and economic prosperity. Early in their school careers, German children feel the pressure to perform well in order to gain access to the three-tier school system – Hauptschule, Realschule, and Gymnasium (Hauptschule for the worst education achievers, and Gymnasium being for the top achievers). Attending a Gymnasium, which leads to higher education entrance qualifications and greater career opportunities, is seen as a sign of individual achievement and a symbol of social advancement and recognition.

Historical Roots and the Humboldtian Educational Ideal

The appreciation for education in Germany has deep historical roots. Education was already highly valued in the late Middle Ages, and Johannes Gutenberg's invention of the printing press in the 15th century reinforced this trend. The mass production of books democratized access to knowledge and promoted literacy and intellectual development in Germany.

In the early 19th century, Wilhelm von Humboldt had a lasting impact on the German educational ideal. He believed that education should impart more than just professional skills – it should shape the whole personality, promote critical thinking, and make us responsible citizens of a democratic society. This ideal of comprehensive general education remains an integral part of German culture to this day.

Equal Opportunities Through Free Access to Education

An important expression of the high value placed on education is the virtually free access to educational institutions in Germany. Public schools, universities, and vocational schools are either free or charge only minimal fees. This principle of educational equity ensures that everyone, regardless of social background or financial situation, has the opportunity to reach their full potential.

Public libraries and educational centers also play a central role in German educational culture. They offer a wealth of resources and programs that give people of all ages the opportunity to further their education and grow personally.

A Nation of Books

The love of the written word has a long tradition in Germany. As early as the 15th century, Johannes Gutenberg revolutionized the world with his invention of the printing press. Suddenly, books could be produced in large quantities, which made access to knowledge and education possible for broad sections of the population. Germany became a pioneer in a new era of enlightenment and intellectual progress.

Cities such as Frankfurt and Leipzig developed into vibrant centers of the book trade. The Frankfurt Book Fair, whose roots go back to the 15th century, is today one of the largest and most important international events in the publishing world. Leipzig, affectionately known as the "City of Books," was also an important hub of European publishing until the 20th century.

In the 18th and 19th centuries, most books worldwide were sold in German. It is therefore no wonder that Germany became one of the countries with the highest book holdings per capita. In many private German homes, you can find almost an entire library full of books. This passion for books and the written word continues to shape German culture today and is reflected in the high value placed on education and lifelong learning.

15. KNOWLEDGE SOCIETY

Lifelong Learning as a Cultural Principle

In Germany, education does not end with graduation. Education is seen as a lifelong process that must be continuously nurtured and expanded. Many Germans regularly participate in continuing education courses – whether professionally or privately – to adapt to the changing times or to deepen personal interests. This culture of lifelong learning is supported by a wide range of adult education centers and continuing education institutions.

Employers in Germany also attach great importance to the further training of their employees to ensure that they can keep up with the changing demands of the market and that companies remain innovative.

Education as a Driving Force for Progress and Innovation

The German appreciation for education is a driving force behind the country's economic success and innovative strength. Well-educated and flexible workers form the backbone of the German economy and make it possible to remain competitive in a globalized world.

For Germans, education is far more than a personal advantage – it is the key to a better future for all.

15.2. Critical Thinking

Critical thinking is deeply rooted in German values. It represents the ability to carefully and objectively analyze, question, and make informed decisions about information, assumptions, and arguments. Critical thinking means recognizing prejudices, drawing logical conclusions, and considering alternative perspectives. This value is closely linked to the Enlightenment, an intellectual movement that has profoundly shaped Germany.

Enlightenment and The Birth of Critical Thinking

Germany occupies a central place in the history of the Enlightenment, that epoch that had a lasting impact on 17th and 18th century Europe. German philosophers such as Immanuel Kant, Gottfried Wilhelm Leibniz, and Moses Mendelssohn made significant contributions to the development of this movement, particularly in the areas of reason, science, and ethics.

At the heart of the Enlightenment was the conviction that human reason is the key to knowledge and to shaping a better society. Kant, one of the most influential thinkers of the German Enlightenment, emphasized in his "Critique of Pure Reason" the role of reason as the source of all knowledge. He called on people to use their reason to overcome prejudices, superstitions, and outdated traditions. His famous motto *"Sapere aude"* ("Dare to know") became the guiding principle of the Enlightenment and encouraged people to break away from irrational authorities and develop their own thinking.

The Primacy of Science and the Freedom of Thought

The Enlightenment produced two central principles that continue to shape German thinking today: the primacy of science over religion or ideology and the freedom to ask critical questions and engage in open debate. The Enlightenment encouraged people to question religion and use scientific findings as the basis for their worldview. It promoted a culture of open dialogue and critical engagement.

Rationality and Openness in Everyday Life

This Enlightenment tradition has led to widespread acceptance of scientific findings and a deep-rooted rationality in Germany. In science, facts are paramount, not morals or ideology. Scientific findings and methods are the basis for progress and innovation. Of course, morality plays an important role in society, but the Enlightenment teaches us to distinguish between moral values and scientific facts. Facts must be accepted even if they contradict certain ideologies.

Germans value science and attach great importance to a clear distinction between facts and opinions. They are open to new things and willing to question their opinions in the face of new facts. The scientific method, which is based on critical examination and constant questioning, is deeply ingrained in the German way of thinking.

The Enlightenment in Danger: When Inconvenient Truths are Concealed

Despite the rational mindset, there is a worrying trend in Germany not to openly discuss certain topics, even though they are scientifically proven. One example is the disproportionate representation of certain migrant groups in crime statistics, especially in violent crimes. Although these facts are scientifically proven, they are often concealed so as not to encourage xenophobia.

The situation is similar with the increased mortality rates after the COVID-19 pandemic. Statistics show that mortality was higher after the pandemic than during it, and there are reports of health damage caused by the Covid vaccination. However, public discussion about this remains subdued, and the voices of scientists who are critical of mRNA vaccines are often suppressed.

Another sensitive topic is the biological differences between men and women in terms of cognitive abilities, behavior, and susceptibility to disease. These scientifically sound differences are often ignored for fear of being perceived as sexist.

Elite and Ordinary Citizens: A Conflict Between Control and Enlightenment

In Germany, a growing conflict is emerging between controlling public discourse and the principles of the Enlightenment. This conflict reflects a profound discrepancy between two camps: the elites in politics, media, and large corporations on the one hand, and ordinary citizens on the other.

There seems to be a tendency among the elites to steer public discourse and make certain topics taboo. Uncomfortable truths are often concealed or downplayed, which makes open and honest debate difficult. One example is crime statistics, which show that certain migrant groups are disproportionately involved in violent crime. Out of concern that such facts could lead to false conclusions or xenophobic reactions, this information is often not communicated transparently.

On the other hand, many ordinary German citizens remain true to the ideals of the Enlightenment and freedom of expression. For them, scientific findings and facts are neutral and should not be distorted or censored by moral or ideological

15. KNOWLEDGE SOCIETY

constraints. They reject any form of paternalism and demand an open and honest discourse based on facts and offering space for critical questions.

Critical thinking continues to be an essential part of German values. Despite challenges, the pursuit of rational and objective thinking remains strong. Society encourages asking uncomfortable questions and addressing difficult topics. This openness shows that the principles of the Enlightenment are still valued in Germany.

15.3. Innovation

Germany has been and continues to be a center of technological advancement and innovation. Particularly in the 19th and 20th centuries, groundbreaking inventions revolutionized the country and changed the world. Even today, innovation and progress are firmly anchored in German culture and economy – they are the driving force of a nation that stands for quality and excellence.

German Pioneers and Their Inventions

Germany's history of innovation is rich in inventions that have shaped the world significantly. Around 1440, Johannes Gutenberg ushered in a revolution of knowledge with the invention of the printing press, which dramatically expanded access to knowledge for broad sections of the population. In 1886, Karl Benz set a milestone in mobility with the first practical automobile, forever changing the way people travel. Wilhelm Conrad Röntgen's discovery of X-rays in 1895 revolutionized medicine by allowing doctors to look inside the human body for the first time without opening it.

Albert Einstein changed our understanding of space and time in 1905 with his theories of relativity, creating the foundation for modern technologies such as GPS. Werner Heisenberg and Max Born introduced quantum mechanics in 1925, a revolution in the understanding of matter that significantly influenced our modern electronics. Otto Hahn and Fritz Strassmann discovered nuclear fission in 1938, paving the way for nuclear energy. Finally, Konrad Zuse developed the first computer in 1941, ushering in the digital revolution and establishing the modern information society.

German Innovative Strength in Key Industries

The achievements of these pioneers laid the foundation for Germany's role as a global innovation leader in numerous key industries. In the automotive industry, where brands such as Volkswagen, BMW, and Mercedes-Benz stand for technical brilliance and innovation, Germany has set global standards. The German chemical and pharmaceutical industry was also groundbreaking with discoveries such as the Haber-Bosch process and aspirin. Germany remains a leader in the research and development of new drugs and therapies.

Germany has also set standards in physics and electronics. The development of laser technology, advances in optics, and research into renewable energies are just a few examples of the country's continuous innovative strength. Technologies such as the integrated circuit and the modern microscope, both originating from Germany, have had a lasting impact on science, medicine, and entertainment.

15. KNOWLEDGE SOCIETY

A Culture of Innovation

At the heart of German innovation culture is the deep urge for perfection. Perfection means always striving for the highest quality and precision, whether in product development, engineering, or scientific research.

Curiosity is another fundamental value. In Germany, children are taught from an early age to ask questions and critically question the world. This curiosity promotes creative thinking and forms the foundation for technological progress and originality.

Originality is highly valued in German innovation culture. It is not about copying existing solutions, but about developing unconventional approaches and courageously breaking new ground.

Finally, sustainability plays a central role. Innovations in Germany are designed to provide long-term solutions that benefit both the current generation and future generations. Technological developments must not only be functional but also ecologically and socially sustainable.

Germany in Transition: The New Challenges of Innovation

Despite its impressive history, Germany today faces new challenges. In emerging fields such as artificial intelligence, biotechnology, and digitalization, countries like the USA and China have gained significant ground in recent years. While Germany remains strong in traditional sectors such as the automotive industry, the challenge is to position itself in new technologies to remain internationally competitive. A new innovation push is needed to stay at the forefront in a rapidly changing world.

The future of German innovation depends on how well the country adapts to these new realities and integrates its values of perfection, curiosity, originality, and sustainability into these new areas.

16. LOVE OF NATURE

From romantic walks in the forest to passionate protests for climate protection – the love of nature is deeply rooted in Germany. It is more than just a hobby or leisure activity; it is a deep connection that manifests itself in art, literature, everyday life, and even in the Constitution.

This chapter explores the "green soul" of Germany and how this love of nature shapes people's lives:

- **Connection to Nature:** The deep connection of Germans to nature, rooted in art, literature, and everyday life.
- **Environmental Awareness:** The deep concern for the environment, which is expressed in recycling, energy conservation, and sustainable consumption.
- **Climate Protection:** A race against time to stop global warming.
- **Love of Animals:** The respect and care for animals, from pets to wildlife.

16.1. Connection to Nature

For Germans, nature is not just a resource or a place for leisure activities, but also a source of inspiration and a refuge for the soul. They seem to firmly believe that nature has an intrinsic value that goes beyond its material benefits. This deep connection is rooted in their cultural values and finds expression in their art, literature, and daily lives.

Romanticism: Nature as a Muse

German Romanticism, a cultural movement of the 18th and 19th centuries, idealized nature as a source of beauty, harmony, and spiritual experience. Great poets and painters such as Goethe, Schiller, and Caspar David Friedrich celebrated nature in their works, thereby creating an awareness of its importance that continues to this day. Their paintings and poems brought to life the majestic mountains, the mysterious forests, and the gentle rivers, showing nature as a place of longing and wonder.

Nature as a Source of Strength: Forest Walks and More

This deep connection to nature also shapes the actions of many Germans today. They often prefer camping holidays amidst forests and lakes to the hustle and bustle of cities. They seek peace and relaxation in nature, hike through their beloved forests, enjoy the fresh air and the beauty of the trees. It is as if they find themselves again in nature, leaving the stress of everyday life behind and recharging their batteries.

As a teenager, I often smiled at my grandparents' fondness for long walks in the forest. But over time, I discovered the calming power of the forest for myself. A walk among the trees can be like balm for the soul, reducing stress and restoring inner strength. It is as if nature, with its tranquility and constancy, brings people back into balance.

The Forest as a Study Aid

During my studies near the Teutoburg Forest, the forest was not just a retreat for me, but my learning space. Most of my learning time was spent under the trees, and this environment helped me successfully complete my law degree and state law exams with distinction after only two semesters, while most students take more than 5 years for this. When fellow students asked me how I was able to pass the state exam after only one year of study, I answered: "With the forest!" The silence and concentration I found there enabled me to absorb the knowledge much faster.

When I suggest to my friends abroad: "Let's go for a walk!", they are often baffled: "Where to?" My answer: "In nature, it doesn't matter where." This answer usually results in incredulous looks. "Why walk? We can drive! But you have to know where to go!", I hear then. This surprised reaction comes from the fact that in many countries the concept of a walk in nature is foreign. There you walk to reach a specific destination, not for the sake of walking or nature. For many Germans, however, walking in the forest is an important part of mental health and a way to ground themselves and recharge their batteries.

Protection of Waters

Germans are particularly fond of their rivers and lakes. They are passionately committed to maintaining water quality, supporting renaturation projects, and ensuring that no garbage ends up in nature. Clean waters are much more than just a matter of aesthetics for them – they are the basis for a healthy life. They want their children and grandchildren to be able to bathe in clear lakes and swim in pristine rivers.

Although there is plenty of rain and many rivers in Germany, Germans are particularly careful about protecting their water. Chemicals do not belong in the water – except perhaps a little soap in everyday life. In other countries, I have often seen old medicines simply disposed of in the toilet. For Germans, however, this is an absolute taboo. Furthermore, in Germany, wastewater is not simply discharged unfiltered into the seas or rivers. All wastewater is thoroughly treated before it is returned to the natural water cycle.

The German connection to nature is a living reality that is deeply reflected in their everyday lives and values. They are aware of the responsibility to protect nature in order to preserve its beauty and diversity for future generations.

16.2. Environmental Awareness

Germans are known for their commitment to environmental protection. They see themselves as guardians of their natural resources and pioneers in environmental protection.

The Green Movement: From Germany to the World

This deep-rooted attitude is one of the reasons why the green movement has been so successful in Germany. Environmental protection is a central issue that strongly influences political decisions of the Germans. Ecological issues play a key role in every election. Germans expect their government to take measures to protect the environment.

Recycling: Detectives on the Trail of Valuable Resources

Their thoroughness is also evident in recycling. Waste is meticulously separated, almost like detectives searching for valuable resources. Paper, glass, organic waste, packaging, and residual waste are all neatly sorted, a system that has been perfected over decades and has given Germany one of the highest recycling rates in the world.

In addition, they have introduced two innovative systems: the "Green Dot" and the deposit system. The Green Dot signals that the manufacturer contributes to the disposal and recycling of its packaging.

The deposit system rewards the return of empty bottles and cans. Each bottle and can carries a 25-cent deposit, which is refunded via a voucher when the item is returned to any store that sells it. This simple incentive system ensures that packaging is recycled rather than discarded.

Electronic waste and batteries are also disposed of conscientiously. Once I took old batteries that I couldn't dispose of in an environmentally friendly way in China back to Germany – my Chinese friends couldn't understand that, but for Germans it's a matter of course to make even the smallest contributions to environmental protection.

Saving Energy: Lights Out and Devices Unplugged

Germans are true masters of saving energy. Electronic devices are consistently switched off when not in use, and the lights are switched off immediately when leaving a room.

Saving Water: Every Drop Counts

Their meticulousness is also evident when it comes to saving water. When showering, only as much water is used as necessary, and the tap is not left running unnecessarily when brushing teeth – a cup is used for this purpose. Even when flushing the toilet, they make sure to use only as much water as needed. Every drop is used consciously, in keeping with their sustainable lifestyle.

Sustainable Consumption: Conscious Decisions

Germans focus on quality over quantity and prefer sustainably produced products and regional and seasonal food. Plastic packaging is avoided wherever possible, and companies that are actively committed to environmental protection are supported. Repairing and reusing take precedence over throwing away and replacing.

For Germans, environmental protection is more than just lip service – it is a deeply rooted conviction that shapes their everyday lives. This conviction is evident in their daily decisions, in their political actions, and in their pride in their green soul.

16.3. Climate Protection

Germans are deeply concerned about climate protection. Discussions and efforts for a more sustainable future are omnipresent, and many people see it as their responsibility to actively contribute to protecting the planet.

Fridays for Future

The "Fridays for Future" movement has gained impressive momentum in Germany and is a striking symbol of the younger generation's commitment. Every Friday students and young people take to the streets in droves to fight vociferously for more ambitious climate policies. Their demands aim for a radical reduction in CO_2 emissions and other greenhouse gases to curb global warming. This young generation is aware of its responsibility for the future and is prepared to stand up resolutely for the protection of the planet. But it is not only the young – almost every German is committed to climate protection.

Motivation: From Personal Fears to Global Responsibility

The motivation behind this commitment is diverse. Many Germans are already seeing the effects of climate change in their own country: heat waves, droughts, and floods are becoming more frequent, and extreme weather events are threatening livelihoods. At the same time, they recognize their global responsibility. Poorer countries in the Global South, which have contributed little to climate change, are particularly hard hit by its consequences. Rising sea levels that are making islands disappear, drought areas that are turning fertile land into uninhabitable land, and water scarcity that is triggering conflict and migration – all of this is already a reality for millions of people.

Climate Ideologues vs. Climate Rationalists: A Battle of Ideas

In Germany, there is broad agreement that climate change is real and that human activities are contributing to it. But there are different views on the causes and the best solutions. This conflict is particularly evident between the so-called "climate ideologues" and the "climate rationalists."

The "climate ideologues" see climate change as an immediate, existential threat and demand drastic measures. They advocate for an immediate move away from fossil fuels, a drastic reduction in traffic, and a comprehensive transformation of the economy. Some activists, such as the "Klimakleber" ("climate stickers,") even go so far as to glue themselves to roads to block traffic and draw attention to their demands.

The "climate rationalists," on the other hand, share the concern about climate change but take a more pragmatic approach. They focus on technology-oriented solutions that take into account both economic realities and global contexts. A central criticism of this group is the strong focus on German CO_2 emissions, although Germany is responsible for less than 2% of global emissions. While emissions in Germany have decreased in the last 30 years, global emissions, especially in countries like China, have increased significantly.

This is impressively illustrated in the following graph:

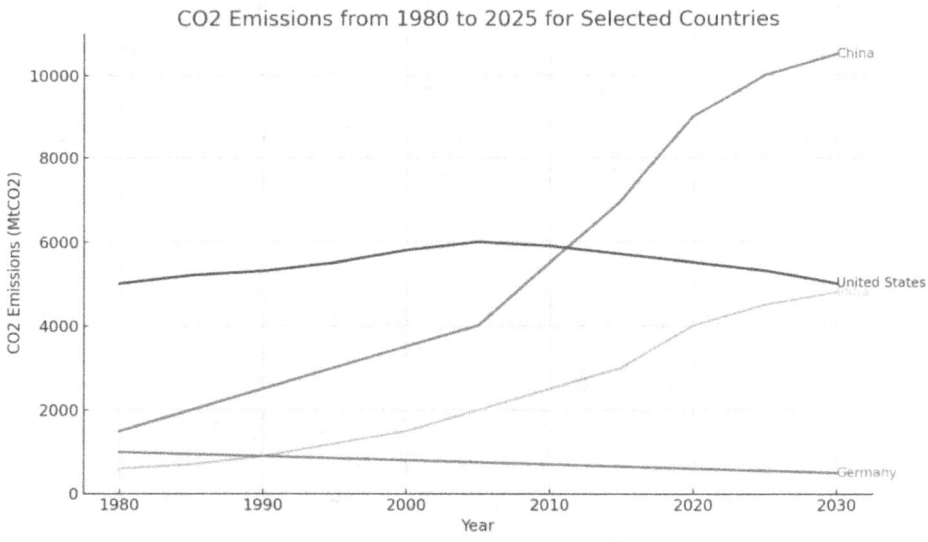

In the 1960s and 1970s, Germany was responsible for about 15% of global CO2 emissions, but today, that figure has dropped to less than 2%. In contrast, China's share has surged from 5% to nearly 40% during the same period.

The "climate rationalists" argue that shifting industrial production from Germany to countries with less stringent environmental regulations and lower energy costs ultimately leads to a global increase in emissions. They view this as a

16. LOVE OF NATURE

dangerous trend, exacerbated by Germany's high energy prices, which are partly the result of government climate policies. For them, this creates a vicious cycle: Germany's deindustrialization would not only bring economic disadvantages but also harm the climate, as production shifts to countries with lower environmental standards.

Climate Protection in Daily Life

Despite differing opinions on the best approach to climate protection, one consensus remains strong in Germany: everyone must do their part. And this is reflected in daily actions, both small and large. Germans burn only clean fuels like gas, wood, or paper, avoiding materials like plastic or tires that release toxic and climate-damaging gases.

In other countries, I've often seen old car tires or plastic waste being burned. In Germany, however, even burning freshly cut wood or wood that's been soaked by rain is strictly prohibited! The reason is simple: Moist wood releases significantly more pollutants, including harmful polycyclic aromatic hydrocarbons (PAHs). That's why German law requires that wood must be dried for at least one year to ensure it's properly dry before it can be burned at all.

Households are mindful of energy-efficient heating practices. When airing out rooms, windows are opened only briefly to minimize heat loss. Even showers are kept short, using lukewarm water to save both energy and water.

For short distances, the bicycle is a preferred mode of transport, not only reducing emissions but also enhancing the quality of life in cities. Air travel and cruises are increasingly viewed critically, and many, especially younger generations, offset the high CO2 emissions from such trips through voluntary contributions to climate protection projects.

These behaviors reflect a deeply rooted environmental consciousness and a commitment to taking responsibility for one's carbon footprint. In Germany, climate protection is not just a political issue but a personal conviction that is expressed in the everyday lives of its people.

16.4. Animal Love

Germans have a deep sense of responsibility towards nature and its creatures. For them, animals are not just cute companions or livestock, but sentient beings that deserve respect and protection. This attitude is firmly anchored in their cultural values and is reflected both in their daily actions and in their laws.

Pets: Part of the Family

Germans consider pets to be full members of their families. They share their homes with them, take care of their well-being, and invest time, money, and energy to ensure they have a happy life. If they see a pet being neglected or abused, they do not hesitate to inform the authorities to help the animal. This love of animals knows no bounds.

Love of Animals Beyond Borders

This love of animals is not limited to their own country. German tourists often care for stray dogs and cats abroad, take them to the vet, or look after them where needed. Locals in other countries sometimes find that Germans care almost as much about animals as they do about people. These observations show how deeply rooted this love of animals is in German culture.

Respect for Wild Animals and Their Habitat

Germans also have respect for wild animals and their natural habitat. They know that wild animals are essential to the ecosystem and must be protected to preserve biodiversity. Germans strictly adhere to hunting and fishing rules to ensure the protection of animals and their habitats. Even if Germans encounter a spider in their home, the animal is not killed, but carefully brought outside to enable it to live safely in nature.

Animal Abuse: An Absolute No-Go

Animal cruelty is strictly rejected in Germany. As soon as Germans witness animal cruelty, they report it to the authorities and advocate for the punishment of the perpetrators. In addition, they prefer meat and dairy from farms that treat their animals well, even if these are more expensive. In German supermarkets, meat producers have been labeling their products with a scale of 1 to 4 according to species-appropriate husbandry for quite some time. Since only 3 or 4 points attest to truly animal-friendly husbandry, Germans who are familiar with the point system only buy such products. Meat with 1 or 2 points in animal husbandry is avoided by consumers.

The Ideologues and the Rationalists: Two Camps of Animal Love

Despite the shared love of animals, there are two camps in Germany when it comes to animal welfare: the ideologues and the rationalists. The ideologues would never harm an animal and believe that animals should have almost the same basic rights as humans. For them, protecting an animal often takes precedence over economic interests. An example of this is the case in Tübingen, where the expansion of a hospital serving 3 million people was stopped due to the sighting of one rare bird – the European Nightjar. Although the bird has not been sighted for over a year, the ideologues continue to demand measures to protect it and therefore prohibit the expansion of the hospital.

The rationalists, on the other hand, weigh animal life against other values. They also do not want to harm any animal but recognize that human interests must be taken into account. For them, animal welfare is not paramount but must be weighed in context.

A Heart for Animals

Germans agree that every living being deserves respect and dignity. Their love of animals is an expression of their humanity and their sense of responsibility towards nature. They advocate that animals are not exploited or abused, but can live in dignity, and act accordingly – whether by buying products from species-appropriate husbandry, protecting wild animals, or treating pets with care.

17. SUSTAINABILITY

Sustainability is a deeply rooted attitude towards life in Germany, reflected in many facets of German culture and everyday life. While the term is often used synonymously with environmental friendliness today, its meaning goes far beyond that. Sustainability means making decisions that consider not only the here and now but also the long-term effects.

This chapter highlights three central aspects of this comprehensive sustainability:

- **Thriftiness**: A conscious use of resources and price-conscious consumer behavior.
- **Modesty**: A lifestyle based on inner values instead of displaying wealth.
- **Long-term thinking**: Germans think about the future when planning finances and designing political and economic systems.

17.1. Thriftiness

Germans are known for their deep-rooted thriftiness.

Proverbs as a Mirror of the German Soul

The German language is rich in proverbs that emphasize the value of thriftiness and financial responsibility. Sayings like *"Spare in der Zeit, dann hast du in der Not"* ("Save in good times, so you have in times of need") encourage foresight, while *"Wer den Pfennig nicht ehrt, ist des Talers nicht wert"* ("Who does not honor the penny is not worthy of the dollar") underlines the importance of small amounts. These wisdoms, passed down from generation to generation, embody a collective attitude towards life that sees thriftiness as the key to a secure and fulfilling life.

Price-Conscious Consumption

German consumers are known for their price-conscious attitude. They compare prices, take advantage of special offers, and make sure to get the best value for money. However, thriftiness does not mean sacrificing quality. On the contrary: Germans prefer to invest in durable, high-quality products that will provide pleasure for years to come rather than cheap goods that have to be replaced quickly.

The "Repair Culture": Sustainability and Appreciation

A striking example of this mentality is the "repair culture." Instead of simply throwing away defective items, Germans prefer to repair them and give them a new life. Whether it's a bicycle, kitchen appliance, or shoes – they appreciate the value of things and are proud to repair them themselves. This attitude not only protects their wallets but also the environment and testifies to a deep respect for the resources that have gone into manufacturing products.

Food Waste: An Attack on the German Soul

Waste, especially of food, is deeply abhorrent to Germans. They carefully plan purchases and meals to avoid waste and creatively use leftovers. Even in restaurants, they only order as much as they can actually eat. This attitude is an expression of thriftiness and respect for the farmers and nature that provide this food.

Financial Provision and Planning

For Germans, thriftiness means not only consuming as few resources as possible but also providing for the future. Financial provision is a cornerstone of the German mentality. They save for unforeseen expenses, major purchases, and retirement, always mindful of stability and security. This mindset is also reflected in politics: the introduction of the debt ceiling, which limits new government debt, is an expression of the deeply rooted desire for financial responsibility.

For Germans, thriftiness is more than just a means of saving money – it is an expression of responsibility and strength of character. Thriftiness stands for a sustainable, balanced lifestyle that benefits both present and future generations.

17.2. Modesty

Germans are known for their deep-rooted modesty. Modesty is not just a cliché or a stereotypical attribution, but a living part of their identity that is reflected in their language, behavior, and institutions.

Historical Roots of Modesty

Christianity has shaped German culture for centuries and has anchored modesty as a virtue. Christian teachings emphasize humility and contentment and warn against the dangers of materialism. Jesus' words *"Es ist leichter, dass ein Kamel durch ein Nadelöhr geht, als dass ein Reicher ins Reich Gottes gelangt"* ("It is easier for a camel to go through the eye of a needle than for a rich man to enter the kingdom of God") urge restraint in the pursuit of wealth and direct the focus to the true values of life. Martin Luther's Reformation reinforced these principles by emphasizing hard work, thrift, and the avoidance of waste.

Prussian history has also deeply ingrained modesty in Germany. Frederick William I, King of Prussia in the 18th century, exemplified strict frugality, which stood in stark contrast to the lavish lifestyle of other monarchs. With his famous saying *"Ich bin der erste Diener meines Staates"* ("I am the first servant of my state"), he underlined the values of a sense of duty and modesty, which are still valued in German culture today.

Consumer Behavior: Quality over quantity

The consumer behavior of Germans is characterized by modesty. They buy consciously, weigh carefully, and make purchasing decisions based on need, quality, and durability. Spontaneous purchases are alien to them; instead, they appreciate timeless, classic products that do not follow every short-lived fashion trend.

Understatement instead of Boasting

Instead of flaunting wealth, Germans cultivate understatement so as not to attract attention or elevate themselves above others. While in the USA the saying "Keeping up with the Joneses" describes wanting to keep up with the material standards of one's neighbors, in Germany one could rather speak of "Keeping down with the Joneses." Prosperity is presented discreetly so as not to give the impression that one has more than one's neighbor.

Germans work hard to earn money but spend it thoughtfully. Money is not an end in itself but a means to a good and secure life. Instead of spending it on short-lived trends or status symbols, they prefer to invest in long-term values such as education, retirement provision, or real estate. This attitude is deeply rooted in the culture and historical heritage.

Wasting Money: An Absolute Taboo

Wasting money is frowned upon in Germany. Even wealthy people prefer to drive a solid family car rather than a flashy luxury car. Spending money on superfluous luxury is considered inappropriate.

An example of this is the public outrage when footballer Franck Ribéry ate a gold-covered steak in Dubai – a behavior that drew sharp criticism in Germany. Ribéry couldn't understand the fuss, as he had merely spent his own money and hadn't harmed anyone. However, he had violated something much deeper: the German ideal of modesty and the intolerance towards the extravagant display of wealth.

For Germans, modesty is more than just a virtue. It is an expression of good taste and a sense of responsibility. It stands for a sustainable, balanced lifestyle that benefits both the people themselves and future generations.

17.3. Long-term Thinking

Long-term thinking is deeply rooted in German culture and manifests itself in many aspects of daily life. It is not just about making plans, but about always making decisions with a view to their future impact.

Looking Beyond the Here and Now

A particularly clear example of this long-term thinking is the German attitude towards finances. Germans attach great importance to regularly setting aside part of their income to be prepared for the future. This prudence provides a sense of security and a willingness to cope with major expenses or unexpected events without stress.

While in countries such as Spain, the United Kingdom, or the USA only between 5 and 8% of monthly income is saved, the savings rate in Germany is on average an impressive 15%. This clearly shows how prudently Germans plan their finances and focus on long-term security.

This is illustrated in the following graph:

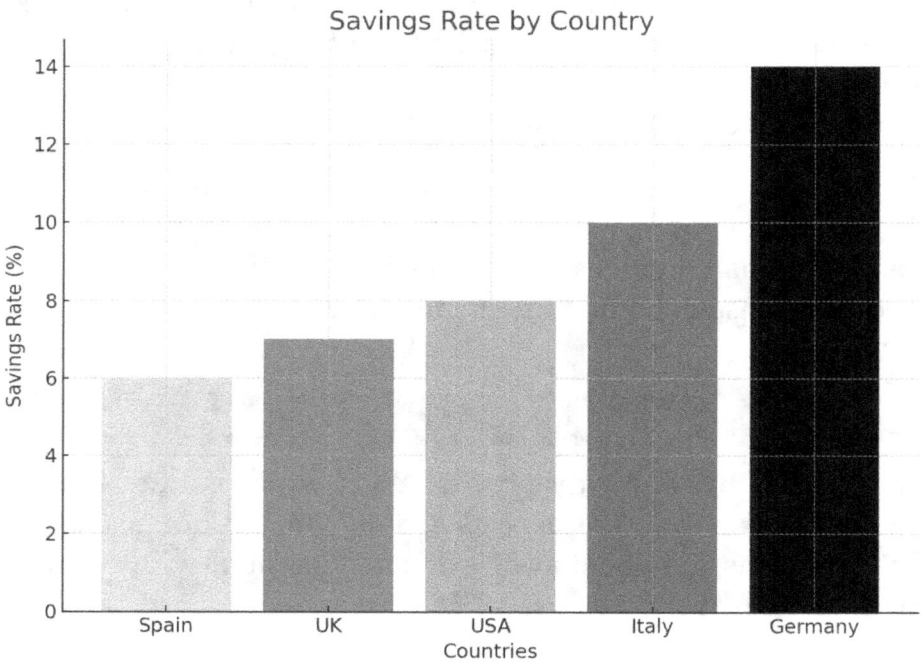

17. SUSTAINABILITY

Many Germans start paying systematically into their retirement provision at a young age. Retirement provision has a high priority, and many people think about how much they will receive in old age early on. A good example of this forward-looking thinking is the widespread home savings contract ("Bausparvertrag"), which aims to save early on for the purchase of a home and build up assets in the long term.

This early financial provision distinguishes Germans from many other cultures where the focus is more on living in the moment. While in other countries the present enjoyment often takes priority, Germans are prepared to make sacrifices today in order to enjoy financial security and prosperity tomorrow.

Focus on Quality and Sustainability

Long-term thinking is also evident in everyday German life. Vacation trips are often planned well in advance to ensure that everything runs smoothly and the best possible experience is achieved. Likewise, large projects, such as building a house or organizing family celebrations, are prepared with great foresight to ensure long-term success.

This way of thinking is also reflected in consumer decisions: quality is preferred to quantity. Germans prefer to invest in durable, high-quality products, even if they are initially more expensive. Whether it is a car, a piece of furniture, or a household appliance – the intention is that it will last for many years and thus create added value in the long term.

Politics and Economy: Foresight and Sustainability

Long-term thinking is also deeply rooted in German politics. While political campaigns address current issues, the focus is often on the future. Measures are taken to ensure that Germany remains stable and sustainable in the coming decades. One example is the "Energiewende" (energy transition), which is driving the transition to renewable energies. This initiative requires significant investment and sacrifice by the German population but it is supported to create a better future for generations to come.

The same mindset is evident in business, especially in medium-sized and family businesses. These companies are not striving for quick profits, but to preserve and strengthen the company for generations to come. Investments in research, development, and employee training ensure long-term innovation and competitiveness.

Long-term thinking shapes the actions, decisions, and social life of Germans. This foresight is an essential part of the German success culture and ensures that a stable and sustainable society is created that offers future generations a future worth living.

18. LOYALITÄT

Loyalty is a fundamental principle of German values that shapes actions and relationships, whether at work, in the family, or in the circle of friends. Germans believe in the power of lasting bonds and appreciate the security and trust they offer. For them, loyalty means being there for each other, in good times and bad.

This chapter highlights three central aspects of this deep-rooted loyalty:

- **Company loyalty**: Germans often remain loyal to their employers for many years.
- **Relationship loyalty**: Germans invest time and energy in building lasting friendships and partnerships.
- **Bindingness:** Germans take their commitments seriously, even before they have formally entered them.

18.1. Company Loyalty

In Germany, company loyalty, i.e., loyalty to one's employer, is an outstanding characteristic that distinguishes German employees and forms a strong contrast to many other work cultures. While in some countries frequent job changes are seen as a normal career step, German employees often remain loyal to their employer for many years.

Loyalty and Faithfulness in German Working Life

While employees in the USA stay with the same employer for an average of only four years, German employees remain loyal to their company for an impressive 10.5 years. This high average length of employment speaks for a deep-rooted loyalty and long-term bond between employers and employees.

As the graph below shows, Germany has the longest average length of employment in international comparison. This underlines the special importance of loyalty and long-term commitment in German working life.

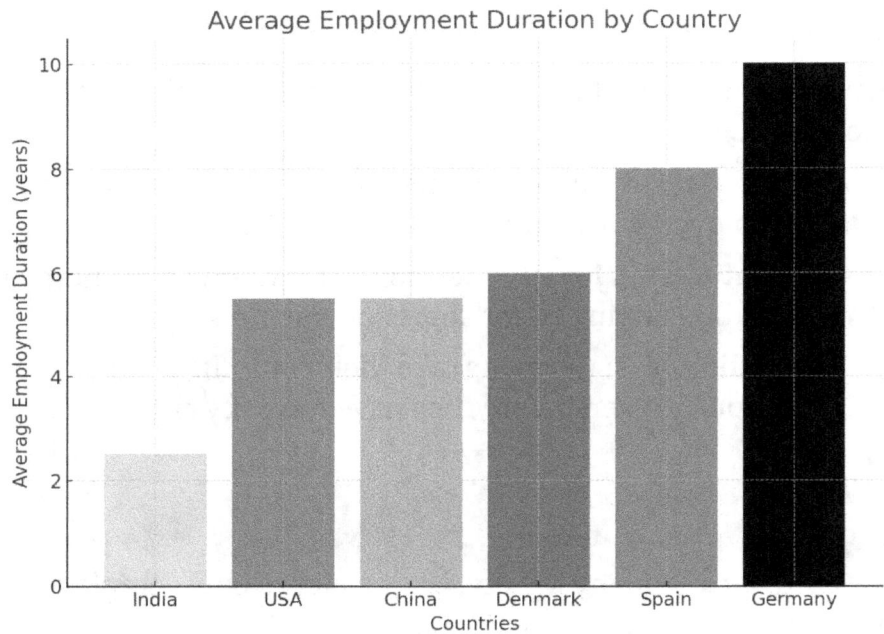

In Germany, it is common for employers to comprehensively care for the well-being of their employees. This is reflected in company pension schemes and a wide range of training opportunities. In return, employees show a strong commitment to their company and often remain loyal to it for many years, even when more attractive offers beckon.

Personal Experiences with Loyalty

I have experienced the loyalty of German employees firsthand. You don't have to worry that a German employee will immediately throw in the towel and resign at the first disappointment, such as a disagreement or misunderstanding. Even being poached by competing companies offering higher salaries is rare among German employees.

This is in stark contrast to my experiences with employees from other cultures, where I have often seen employees switch jobs immediately as soon as they receive a more attractive offer from a competitor.

There have also been cases where employees were working on a promising project and used this knowledge to set up a competing business - sometimes even taking trade secrets or programming code with them to compete with their former employer.

In Germany, this is extremely rare. German employees strongly identify with their employer and remain loyal.

This company loyalty is a central component of German work culture and contributes significantly to the stability and success of German companies. It enables long-term planning, promotes the development of expertise and experience, and creates a climate of trust.

18.2. Relationship Loyalty

Germans are not only loyal and steadfast in their jobs, but also in their private lives. Faithfulness in relationships is a central value that plays a significant role in both marriages and friendships. They believe in the power of lasting bonds and appreciate the trust and security they offer.

Friendships for Life

While many cultures cultivate superficial acquaintances and celebrate the good times, Germans are about more than just partying together. They may be a bit hesitant to make new friends, but once you've made it into their inner circle, you've gained a friend for life. And that means: They are not only there when the sun is shining, but they also stand by you when things get stormy. Whether it's illness, job loss, or personal crises - you can count on German friends!

Marriage and Partnership for Life

Germans also value faithfulness and commitment in love. Marriage is seen as a serious, long-term relationship. Sure, getting married is not as "in" as it used to be, and divorce is no longer taboo. Nevertheless, Germans do not throw in the towel immediately when problems arise, but work on their relationship. And in fact, marriages in Germany still last a relatively long time on average - about 15 years, while in the USA it's only about 8 years.

Germans are not only geared towards the long term in their jobs, but also in their relationships. For them, it is not just about the short-term thrill, but about the deep connection that survives all the ups and downs of life.

18.3. Bindingness

In Germany, bindingness ("Verbindlichkeit") is a central value that plays a prominent role in both professional and personal relationships. "Verbindlichkeit" ist hard to translate, and bindiness does not capture the full meaning; it means that Germans do not say things casually. Anything a German says, even without a clear agreement, can be counted on.

More than just Reliability: Words Carry Weight

Bindingness goes beyond mere reliability. While reliability means keeping promises, Germans also take casual statements seriously. They feel obligated to fulfill what they have said - even if it was only mentioned in passing. Every word carries weight and is put into action whenever possible.

Experiences from the World of Work

In my experience with hundreds of freelancers worldwide, German workers have always distinguished themselves through their bindingness. They rarely make rash promises, especially not regarding prices or schedules. But when a German finally gives you a price or a timeframe, they mean it.

In other cultures, big promises are often made that are then not kept. "No problem, we can do it, fast and cheap!" is a common refrain. But when push comes to shove, deadlines are postponed, prices are increased, and commitments are broken.

This is particularly noticeable when recruiting talents. Often, after long discussions, we were on the verge of hiring candidates from other countries - and then nothing more happened; they ghosted us. They probably had found a job elsewhere, but instead of letting us know, they simply disappeared. A German would at least have gotten back in touch.

German employers also don't leave applicants in the lurch. Even if you are rejected, you will get a clear answer. Simply disappearing - unthinkable!

Bindingness in Private Life

Germans are also reliable in their private lives. If someone says to you, "Let's meet up sometime," they mean it. Usually, the question follows directly: "When would it suit you?"

Bindingness also means being direct and honest. If a German realizes that they are no longer interested in a friendship or relationship, they will tell you instead of just disappearing. "Ghosting" is considered extremely rude. Even on a dating app, like Tinder, it is still rare that a German will just block you or delete the contact, if they have already exchanged messages.

Bindingness creates trust. You know where you stand and can rely on what has been said. This bindingness is important to German culture and ensures that Germans are considered trustworthy partners internationally.

19. LOVE OF FREEDOM

Love of freedom is a cornerstone of German values. While the chapter on "Pluralism" focused on the importance of individual lifestyle choices, this chapter deals with freedoms that protect opinions, bodily autonomy, personal space, and privacy.

- **Right to bodily autonomy:** Whether regarding medical decisions, the vaccination debate, or abortion – the right to bodily autonomy is a central aspect of personal freedom.
- **Personal space:** Germans value their personal space and respect the space of others.
- **Privacy:** The protection of privacy means freedom from invasion or interference in private affairs.
- **Freedom of speech and freedom of the press:** These freedoms form the foundation of democracy and make it possible to exchange ideas openly and express criticism.

19.1. Bodily Autonomy

In Germany, the right to bodily autonomy is deeply rooted in society and law. It emphasizes that every person has the sovereign right to decide about their own body without the state, institutions, or individuals being allowed to intervene without their consent.

The Principle of Consent

The right to bodily autonomy is particularly evident in the informed consent that precedes any medical treatment. Doctors are obligated to inform you comprehensively about the risks and benefits of a treatment. You then decide independently whether to accept or decline the treatment. This is also why there is no general compulsory vaccination in Germany. No one can be forced to inject a substance into their body.

However, during the Corona pandemic, the fear of the virus led to a de facto restriction of the right to physical self-determination, as many people lost their jobs if they refused to be vaccinated. These measures met with great resistance among the population.

The Right to Abortion

Another example of the importance of bodily autonomy in Germany is abortion law. Abortions are legal in the first 12 weeks of pregnancy, but only after mandatory counseling. This regulation attempts to reconcile a woman's right to self-determination with the protection of the unborn life. The right to bodily autonomy is so important to Germans that in this case it can even outweigh the unborn child's right to life.

Parenting and Physical Integrity

The right to physical integrity is also central in parenting. Corporal punishment of children is prohibited by law in Germany, and even minor "slaps in the face" can lead to police action. This underlines the importance of protecting physical integrity, even in the family and school environment.

Division in Society

However, there are different opinions in Germany regarding bodily autonomy. There are two dominant camps: the social-progressive and the liberal-conservative. Social progressives emphasize the unrestricted right to bodily autonomy, especially in the abortion debate. They demand that women should have full control over their bodies and see restrictions as patriarchal.

At the same time, many of them were prepared to introduce compulsory vaccination during the Corona pandemic and exclude the unvaccinated, as the welfare of the general public took precedence in their view.

On the other side are the liberal-conservatives, who also uphold bodily autonomy, especially when it comes to state control during the pandemic. For them, the protection of personal freedom, even in times of crisis, is an unshakable principle. They strictly reject compulsory vaccination because no one should be forced to introduce something into their body against their will.

Interestingly, many of them are more critical of abortion because they see the unborn child's right to life as a higher good that outweighs the mother's right to bodily autonomy.

Despite these differences, the right to bodily autonomy is an essential cornerstone for both camps and German society as a whole. It is seen as an expression of personal freedom and the dignity of the individual.

19.2 Personal space

Germans have a strong need for personal space. This invisible comfort zone around them is not just a matter of politeness, but an expression of their freedom and self-determination.

Respectful Distance

Forget elaborate greeting rituals with a lot of body contact! A friendly handshake is the norm in Germany and is considered appropriate. Beyond that, Germans are careful to respect other people's personal space and only enter it with their express consent. Hugs, pats on the back, or other physical gestures are usually reserved for close friends or family members.

It is customary to keep a distance of about 60 centimeters from others - a distance that may seem generous by international standards. For Germans, it is a matter of course to maintain this personal zone and not to cross it without being asked.

Public Spaces

In public spaces, Germans make sure to leave as much space as possible between themselves and others. For example, if someone sits on a park bench, they will sit on the opposite side, if possible, to maintain sufficient distance. If the bench is already occupied by two people, they will only sit in the middle after politely asking if it is okay.

Even on crowded buses or trains, they only sit right next to someone if there are no other seats available.

The same principle applies at the swimming pool or on the beach: they make sure to set up their sun lounger as far away from others as possible. If they were to lie down right next to someone, it could be perceived as inappropriate or intrusive.

Consideration in Everyday Life: Distance with Mindfulness

This need for distance is also evident in other everyday situations. In the elevator, Germans stand as far apart as possible and deliberately avoid eye contact in confined spaces to respect the privacy of others. In queues, whether at the supermarket, the bus stop, or the bank, they keep a respectful distance from the person in front of them to avoid feelings of discomfort or crowding.

The need for personal space is deeply rooted in German culture and reflects the value placed on individuality, self-determination, and respect. This space is not only a sign of decency, but also an expression of their love of freedom, which they want to preserve in both their private and public lives.

Germans are known for being masters at respecting privacy. It's as if they have an invisible protective shield around them that they carefully guard and also respect in others.

Discretion is Key: Small Talk Yes, Soul-Striptease No

Germans are not known for asking prying questions, especially not with casual acquaintances. A relaxed small talk about the weather or the last vacation is perfectly fine, but topics like salary, marital status, or age remain taboo. It would be like leafing through someone's diary without being asked - an absolute no-go! Personal information is highly valued, and everyone has the right to decide for themselves what they want to reveal.

The Discreet Gaze

In Germany, there is an unspoken rule that you respect other people's personal space and do not unsettle anyone with intrusive glances.

Imagine you are sitting in a café and see a couple in love kissing tenderly. You instinctively avert your gaze to give them their privacy, at least you should if you are living in Germany. Or you are walking along the beach and see a woman in a bikini sunbathing. Of course, you notice her, but it would never occur to you to stare intrusively. After all, it's none of your business what other people look like or how they dress. Everyone has the right to present themselves as they wish without being watched or judged.

This restraint also applies to people who are different. Whether someone has a visible disability or is very overweight - for Germans, this is no reason to stare or gossip. They treat these people with the same respect and empathy as everyone else.

Even in intimate moments, such as when a young mother is breastfeeding her baby in public, Germans show tact. They deliberately look away to give the mother the necessary privacy. It's about giving other people their space and not unsettling them with looks or comments.

The Golden Rule for Closed Rooms

Whether in the office or at home - Germans do not enter closed rooms without knocking first and waiting for permission. This is a matter of course that shows respect and consideration. After all, no one wants someone to just barge into their private space.

19. LOVE OF FREEDOM

Data Protection and Digital Etiquette

Germans take data protection very seriously; handling someone else's personal information carelessly is unthinkable. However, this respect for privacy isn't universal.

I recently traveled to India and, in need of a SIM card, went into a mobile phone store. As part of the registration, I was asked to present my passport. The employee took one look at it, and his eyes widened – my passport was packed with stamps from countries around the globe. What happened next, though, nearly drove me, a German raised on privacy, up the wall. The employee proceeded to parade my passport through the entire shop, proudly showing it off to everyone, as if having such a well-traveled customer was a badge of honor. I felt my privacy had been invaded and was anything but happy. However, recognizing this as a cultural difference, I managed to stay calm. In Germany, such a display would be out of the question.

Germans also maintain discretion in the digital world. They would never look at the screen of a stranger's smartphone or laptop without being asked. That would be like secretly reading someone's letters. What others do in their free time or who they communicate with is nobody else's business.

Photos: Only with Permission - No Paparazzi Mentality

In Germany, people always ask for permission before taking photos, especially in private or informal situations. And photos of others are only shared with their express consent. Not everyone wants to be captured in a picture, and that is respected. No one should be embarrassed or violated in their privacy by a photo.

For Germans, protecting privacy is not just a matter of etiquette, but an expression of respect and freedom.

19.4. Freedom of Speech

Freedom of speech and freedom of the press are fundamental to democracy, critical thinking, and freedom, and are fortunately deeply anchored in German culture and law.

Constitutional Anchoring

Article 5 of the German Constitution guarantees these rights and states: "Every person shall have the right freely to express and disseminate his opinion by speech, writing, and pictures and freely to inform himself from generally accessible sources. Freedom of the press and freedom of reporting by radio and film shall be guaranteed. There shall be no censorship." This constitutional article is the result of a long historical process and stands as a bulwark against any form of oppression and censorship.

Historical Development of Freedom of Speech

The road to freedom of speech in Germany was long and often marked by setbacks. As early as the 16th century, Martin Luther, with the Reformation, challenged the authority of the Catholic Church, then the most powerful institution in Europe. With his theses, he ignited a revolution that laid the foundation for the idea of freedom of expression.

In the 18th century, Enlightenment thinkers such as Immanuel Kant and Gotthold Ephraim Lessing further advanced the idea of freedom of speech. They emphasized the importance of the

19. LOVE OF FREEDOM

free exchange of thoughts and ideas for social progress. Reason, science, and individuality became central principles of the Enlightenment, which shaped the importance of freedom of expression in Germany.

In the 19th century, the struggle for freedom of speech and the press continued in many German states. The Carlsbad Decrees of 1819 led to censorship and suppression of liberal movements. But resistance grew, and the Revolution of 1848, led by idealistic intellectuals, loudly demanded a constitution, freedom of the press, and the founding of a German nation-state.

Interestingly, this movement linked democracy and freedom of speech with German patriotism. They saw freedom of thought and speech as essential to the flourishing of a united nation.

Nowadays, however, many Germans no longer associate freedom of speech and democracy with nationalism, as they know the 12 years of the Nazi era as a period of nationalism without freedom of speech and without democracy. This historical experience has led many people to equate nationalism with the horrors of an oppressed society, rather than seeing it as a positive force for freedom and self-determination.

Setbacks and Lessons of History

Freedom of speech suffered a severe setback during the Nazi dictatorship. The media was brought into line, and opposition was brutally suppressed. Freedom of the press was also severely restricted in the GDR, and state propaganda dominated.

These experiences have deeply ingrained the value of freedom of speech in the consciousness of Germans. East Germans in particular, who experienced this oppression themselves, appreciate the freedom they have gained all the more.

New Threats to Freedom of Speech

Freedom of speech in Germany today faces new, subtle threats. Politicians and powerful multinational corporations use their influence to exert pressure on social media platforms like YouTube, X (formerly Twitter), and Facebook to censor unwelcome opinions and block accounts. This form of silent censorship endangers democratic debate and can suppress the diversity of opinion.

Recent cases illustrate how quickly freedom of speech can be jeopardized. In my hometown, for example, a young man was recently sentenced to five months in prison without parole for sharing an image on Facebook that was classified as racist.

Another worrying example is the case of German journalist Alina Lipp, who made a documentary in eastern Ukraine. She interviewed residents of Donetsk and Luhansk, and her reporting portrayed the Ukrainian army in a critical light. People expressed their displeasure with the Ukrainian government, and the film gave the impression that many see the Russian army as liberators. Although Lipp did not express her own opinion, she was charged with incitement to hatred, and money was withdrawn from her bank account without warning.

Another example involves a 64-year-old army veteran who reposted an image labeling Robert Habeck, the Minister of the Economy, as a "Schwachkopf" (which translates to "weak-minded" or "idiot"). Following the repost, Habeck filed a lawsuit against the veteran. As a result, the police visited the veteran's home at 6:15 a.m. and confiscated his mobile phone.

19. LOVE OF FREEDOM

Such cases illustrate that freedom of speech in Germany today is under greater pressure than it seems at first glance.

Division Regarding Freedom of Speech

There is a growing division in German society on the issue of freedom of speech: on the one hand, there are the liberals, and on the other, the ideologues.

The German ideologues believe that certain opinions that contradict their ideology are dangerous and have the potential to undermine democracy and freedom of speech. They argue that such views should be suppressed to protect society from perceived threats, as these opinions could lead to the destabilization of democratic values. For them, certain perspectives are not only incorrect but morally reprehensible, and thus should have no place in public discourse. In their view, censoring these dangerous ideas is necessary to maintain a just and harmonious society.

The German liberals (freedom lovers), on the other hand, strongly defend the right to freedom of speech, even when they find opposing views to be incorrect or inappropriate. For them, the diversity of opinions is an indispensable pillar of a healthy democracy. They are convinced that a truly tolerant society must be able to tolerate controversial and even uncomfortable ideas, as these are an integral part of democratic dialogue.

German liberals believe that open debate, rather than suppression, is the best way to challenge dangerous ideas and strengthen democratic principles.

This ideological stance, which seeks to classify certain opinions as inherently dangerous, is currently a minority viewpoint in Germany. However, it is increasingly gaining traction among influential individuals within the establishment—those in the media, politics, the military, and finance—allowing it to exert a growing influence on public policy and discourse.

Despite this, the majority of Germans, particularly ordinary citizens, continue to defend liberal principles and favor a culture of open debate where diverse perspectives can be expressed freely without fear of suppression.

A similar division can be observed in the United States. The American establishment—encompassing the media, politics, the military, and financial sectors—often views Donald Trump, the MAGA movement, and various other voices on the right as threats to democracy and freedom of speech. For that reason they attempt to silence these voices.

In contrast, many ordinary citizens in the U.S. express frustration with the rise of "cancel culture" and the perceived inability to speak freely without facing social or professional consequences. They argue that an environment of self-censorship is stifling open discourse, and that the suppression of controversial opinions undermines the very principles of freedom that democracy is built upon.

This societal divide reflects an ongoing struggle between those who prioritize ideological conformity for the sake of perceived social stability and those who defend the foundational values of free speech and open dialogue and this struggle is common to both Germany and the USA.

Satire and Artistic Freedom

Germans value the freedom of satirists and comedians to make even provocative and controversial jokes. Satire is considered an important part of freedom of expression that allows social

19. LOVE OF FREEDOM

issues to be illuminated in a humorous and critical way. Even though satire can sometimes cross boundaries, in Germany it is understood as a necessary means of artistic freedom that contributes to democratic discourse.

One sign of this tolerance for freedom of expression is that even caricatures of religious figures such as Jesus or Mohammed may be published in Germany. Even though many Germans personally reject these caricatures, the right to publish them is respected as an expression of freedom of the press and freedom of speech.

A tragic example of the tensions that can arise from such expressions of opinion is the deadly attack on the French satirical magazine Charlie Hebdo in 2015 after it published caricatures of Mohammed. There was great sympathy in Germany: many Germans changed their Facebook profile pictures to "Je suis Charlie" (I am Charlie) to express solidarity with the victims. Thousands took to the streets to protest against violence and defend freedom of the press.

Germans condemn any form of violence in response to expressions of opinion. They regard the attack on Charlie Hebdo not only as an attack on individuals, but on the fundamental values of freedom of speech and freedom of the press. They firmly believe that provocation or insult can never justify violence.

Openness to Political Discussions

In Germany, there is a conviction that political statements, even if they are perceived as wrong or immoral, should be tolerated as long as they do not call for violence or illegal activities. It is believed that open discussion about different political systems and ideologies strengthens democratic values.

Engaging with different perspectives and controversial opinions is an essential part of the democratic process.

Germans seek dialogue and promote peaceful debates because they are convinced that such conversations develop and strengthen their society. By respecting these principles, they contribute to an open, tolerant, and democratic society where every voice is heard.

20. PERSONAL RESPONSIBILITY

In Germany, personal responsibility is a deeply rooted principle that shapes people's thinking and actions. For example, if a storm damages a house, Germans often reach for the saw and hammer themselves before asking the state for help. They see this "can-do attitude" as a sign of strength, self-respect, and personal responsibility.

This chapter examines the importance of personal responsibility in Germany:

- **Self-reliance**: Self-initiative and a sense of responsibility characterize Germans.
- **Proactiveness**: Germans think ahead, look for solutions, and drive success, even if something is outside their area of responsibility.
- **Self-respect**: Being able to take care of themselves is important to Germans. They are reluctant to accept help.

20.1. Self-Reliance

Self-reliance is an important value in Germany, running like a common thread through all areas of life. Whether at work, in everyday life, or in society - Germans strive to take their lives into their own hands.

At Work: The Art of Initiative

This pronounced self-reliance is particularly evident in the world of work. Germans prefer to tackle tasks independently rather than constantly relying on detailed instructions or close supervision.

I have admired this self-reliance in German colleagues time and again throughout my career. While in some cultures constant exchange and regular queries are part of everyday working life, I often find German employees to be remarkably independent. They accept tasks, analyze them thoroughly, develop solution strategies, and implement them - often without constant questioning or the need for detailed instructions.

I find it particularly impressive that this self-reliance does not falter even when direct contact is perhaps restricted. You can rely on German employees. They continue to carry out their tasks conscientiously and solve problems independently or at least communicate them clearly.

Self-Organization

Another important aspect of German self-reliance is the ability to self-organize. Germans love to structure their everyday lives, create to-do lists, and use their time efficiently. Setting priorities, effectively managing available time, and making well-considered decisions are skills that are valued in both professional and private life.

From an Early Age: Self-Reliance as an Educational Goal

This appreciation for self-organization and personal responsibility begins in childhood in Germany. From an early age, children are encouraged to structure their everyday lives, do their schoolwork independently, and manage their time efficiently. They are encouraged to make their own decisions and bear the consequences of their actions. This approach is

20. PERSONAL RESPONSIBILITY

intended to help them grow into self-confident and responsible adults.

Fledging: Shaping Your Own Life

After school, it is a natural step for many young Germans to leave their parents' home and start their own lives. This early independence is an important step on the way to adulthood.

In many other Western countries, young people tend to live with their parents for a longer time on average, as the following graphic illustrates:

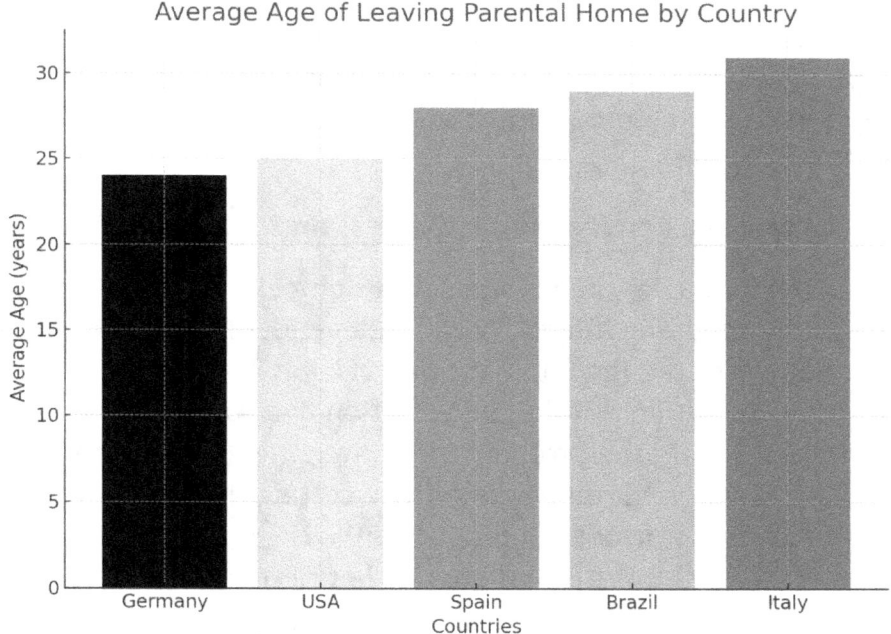

Germans also make their own choices when it comes to major life decisions – whether and when to marry, whether and how many children to have, and which career path to pursue.

This deep-rooted culture of self-reliance and personal responsibility shapes not only individual actions but also society and the economy. It promotes innovation, creativity, and a sense of responsibility and contributes to Germany being a strong and successful nation.

20.2. Proactivity

German employees are not only known for their self-reliance but also for their distinct proactiveness.

While self-reliance describes the ability to complete tasks independently and without constant supervision, proactiveness goes one step further. It encompasses the willingness to think beyond one's own work area and actively look for ways to support the company as a whole.

The Difference Between Proactiveness and Self-Reliance

Proactiveness goes far beyond self-reliance. A simple example: An accountant who diligently and independently completes his work does not require constant supervision. He takes the initiative to obtain missing information and solves minor problems - that is self-reliance. But imagine this accountant realizes through his daily work that a certain division of the company has enormous potential, while the management is planning to sell this division. Instead of remaining silent, he proactively approaches the management and shares his observations, supported by figures and analyses. This enables the management to make an informed decision and potentially avoid a serious mistake: that is proactiveness.

The accountant acts in the interest of the company, even if it is not part of his direct duties. He uses his expertise to advance the company - an attitude that distinguishes many German employees.

A Competitive Advantage: Why Companies Value German Employees

This combination of self-reliance and proactiveness makes German employees an invaluable asset to companies. Even when other countries offer economic advantages such as lower taxes or energy costs, many companies consciously choose Germany. The reason is simple: they know that German employees not only fulfill their duties conscientiously, but also actively seek solutions and further develop the company.

German employees think along, identify challenges early on, and offer solutions without being asked. This work mentality is deeply rooted in German culture and contributes significantly to the international success of German companies.

Proactiveness in Daily Life

German proactivity isn't confined to the workplace; it extends into the everyday lives of Germans. If something needs to be done, they don't stop to question whether it's within their responsibilities—they simply get it done. The guiding principle is: "Just do it."

While cycling through South America, I encountered a traffic jam that stretched for kilometers through the hilly terrain. With my bike, I was able to maneuver past the idle cars and soon discovered the cause: a large branch, knocked down by a storm, lay across one of the lanes, obstructing the flow of traffic. Despite the hundreds of frustrated motorists, no one seemed to be taking action.

It was obvious to me that something had to be done. I parked my bike and started to move the massive branch off the road. In no time, the road was clear, and traffic resumed. This experience highlighted just how ingrained proactiveness is in German culture. In Germany, the idea that so many people would ignore a problem they could easily solve themselves is unimaginable.

Proactiveness: A Key to Success
Proactiveness is a deeply rooted aspect of German culture and plays a crucial role in driving innovation and long-term success. This mindset is one of the reasons why German workers are so highly regarded across the globe and why the German economy remains so competitive.

20.3. Self-Respect

The need to solve one's own problems independently and not to rely on outside help is central to the German self-image. This attitude goes beyond simply overcoming challenges and reflects the belief that it is one's own duty to provide for oneself and one's family.

Reluctance Towards Social Assistance

Seeking Social Assistance? For many Germans, that's a real stumbling block, and it's not just about misplaced pride. Rather, it reflects a deeply ingrained belief: one is responsible for their own well-being and that of their family. This strong sense of personal responsibility shapes the German mentality, leading people to view reliance on state support as a personal failure. It goes against the ideal of independence and "fighting one's own way through."

20. PERSONAL RESPONSIBILITY

As a result, it's not uncommon for people in Germany—despite being eligible for government assistance—to hesitate before accepting it. They strive to stand on their own feet again as quickly as possible, even if it means tightening their belts or taking on multiple jobs simultaneously. This sense of "shame" around social aid runs deep.

This reluctance is especially pronounced in older generations. For many of them, it's a matter of honor not to be a "burden" on society. Having often experienced the hardships of war and scarcity, they value the ability to navigate life through their own efforts.

This mentality even extends to insurance benefits. Personally, I've been privately insured for over 20 years and have always paid for medical bills and medications out of pocket to avoid burdening the collective.

In Germany, social assistance is seen as a last resort, to be used only in absolute necessity.

Differences in Self-Reliance

Since it is a matter of self-respect for many Germans to take personal responsibility for their livelihood and to only make use of state benefits in an absolute emergency, many are outraged that a very high percentage of undocumented immigrants to Germany receive social benefits, especially Bürgergeld (citizen's allowance).

Due to the different attitudes towards self-reliance, 47% of citizen's allowance recipients in Germany are foreigners, and even more, 62%, were not born in Germany. In federal states such as Hamburg, Baden-Württemberg, and Hesse, the proportion of recipients not born in Germany is even over 70%.

These people often receive more support than Germans who have worked for the country all their lives and whose ancestors have built up Germany with great effort over generations and, out of pride or self-respect, have often not claimed state aid, although they would have been entitled to do so.

In recent years, this has unfortunately led to more and more Germans saying: "Before others enrich themselves at the expense of the state and there is nothing left, I would rather claim my share." This has led to a decline in self-reliance, while the desire to maximize one's own advantage has increased.

Reluctance to Borrow Money

The importance of self-reliance in Germany is also reflected in attitudes towards money – and especially debt. While Germans are generally helpful and willing to support others, many find it difficult to ask for help themselves, particularly when it comes to borrowing money.

In my own experience, I've lent money to many acquaintances. What I've noticed is that German friends always make a strong effort to repay the loan as quickly as possible. In other cultures, I've often seen debts linger for much longer.

This observation highlights a typical German characteristic: the desire to be independent and not feel indebted to others. Debt is often seen as a kind of "blemish" that needs to be erased as quickly as possible. Germans would rather go without or tighten their belts than be beholden to someone else.

Self-respect and the pursuit of independence are central values in German value culture. They are reflected in the reluctance to accept social assistance and the endeavor to settle financial obligations quickly. These principles are an expression of strength, responsibility, and the deep conviction that everyone must take care of their own life and that of their family.

21. GOOD MANNERS

From respectful greetings to refined table manners – the art of politeness is deeply rooted in German values and reflects respect and consideration.

A vivid example of the importance of good manners is provided by the film "Borat." In this film, a man from Kazakhstan travels to the USA. Borat is lovable – warm-hearted, open, and friendly. However, his eccentric and uncouth manners repeatedly lead to misunderstandings and irritation. The people he meets may like him, but they feel a certain distance because his behavior does not conform to common social norms.

The situation is similar in Germany when migrants or newcomers have not yet internalized the local social norms. As with Borat, one senses that many newcomers have good hearts, but it is noticeable when they do not master German manners – which occasionally creates a subtle distance.

This chapter invites you to discover the world of good manners in Germany:

- **Polite communication**: The art of choosing words and gestures in a way that promotes harmonious coexistence.
- **Polite behavior**: Subtle but significant rules of conduct that are particularly valued in Germany.
- **Table manners**: The etiquette of eating, especially in formal settings.
- **Well-groomed appearance**: Clean, tidy clothing and personal hygiene as an expression of respect.

21. GOOD MANNERS

21.1. Polite Communication

In Germany, politeness is a finely tuned ballet of words and gestures. To truly belong in Germany and build good relationships, it is important to master the subtle nuances of polite communication.

"Please," "Thank You," and "Excuse Me"

The classics "please," "thank you," and "excuse me" are still indispensable today, whether in private or business life. They are like the oil that keeps the gears of social interaction running smoothly. A simple "please" when asking someone for something shows that you respect the other person and do not take their help for granted.

If Germans accidentally bump into someone or cause inconvenience, they apologize immediately. They thereby show that they recognize and regret their misconduct.

Germans say "thank you" for every favor. It expresses their appreciation and shows that they are aware of the other person's efforts. The usual response is a friendly "You're welcome" or "My pleasure." Direct eye contact is important to underline sincerity.

But gratitude can also be expressed nonverbally. In traffic, Germans thank each other with a nod, a brief tap of the headlights, or a raised hand. Such gestures contribute to a positive climate in everyday life.

Gesundheit! - A Small Greeting With a Big Impact

A loud "hatschi!" (German equivalent of "achoo") sounds, and as a matter of course, a heartfelt "Gesundheit!" ("Bless you!")

follows - not only towards friends and acquaintances, but often also towards complete strangers.

Imagine: You are sitting silently in a full train compartment, everyone lost in their thoughts. Suddenly, a sneeze breaks the silence. And the ice is broken: a "Gesundheit!" here, a "Gesundheit!" there, and before you know it, a lively conversation develops between the passengers.

This simple "Gesundheit!" is so popular that it has even made the leap across the Atlantic. In the USA, it is no longer uncommon for Americans to exclaim a cheerful "Gesundheit!" instead of the traditional "Bless you."

And what if you have to sneeze yourself? There are clear rules in Germany. Traditionally, you hold your hand in front of your mouth to contain the spread of germs. But since the Corona pandemic, a new etiquette has been established: instead of the hand, the crook of the arm is now preferred. After all, a damp, virus-laden hand can quickly become a germ spreader.

"Sie" and "Du" : Two Forms of "You"

Choosing the correct form of address is an important aspect of politeness in Germany. The formal "Sie" is the standard form of address for adults you do not know well. It creates a respectful distance and shows that you respect the other person's boundaries.

The informal "Du," on the other hand, is only used after mutual consent and signals a closer, more personal relationship. In business, there are certain rules about who can offer the "Du" to whom. As a rule, it is the higher-ranking person, the older person, or the woman who takes the initiative and offer the other person to call each other by the informal "Du".

Greeting: The German Handshake

The handshake is an integral part of greeting and also saying goodbye for Germans. A firm handshake with an upright posture, eye contact, and a smile exudes self-confidence and openness.

During the COVID-19 pandemic, the fist bump gained popularity, especially in hygienic situations or casual encounters.

Hugs are common among friends, but in Germany, people do not kiss each other on the cheek as a greeting, as they do in many southern European countries. This physical distance should not be understood as unfriendliness, but as respect for privacy.

Small Talk: Breaking the Ice with Tact

Small talk is an important social skill in Germany to break the ice and create a pleasant atmosphere. It is a way of approaching each other without having to have deep conversations right away. Popular topics are the weather, current events, local events, or common interests.

But certain topics are absolute taboos in Germany, especially if you don't know your counterpart well. These include conversations about the toilet, sex, or feces. These topics are too intimate and can quickly cause discomfort.

Politeness in Germany is more than just a means of avoiding conflict – it is an expression of decency, humanity, and the pursuit of harmony in social interaction.

21.2. Polite Behavior

In Germany, politeness plays a central role in daily interactions and encompasses not only language but also behavior. There are certain behaviors that Germans find particularly inappropriate – faux pas that should be avoided at all costs so as not to attract negative attention.

Farting in Public: An Absolute No-Go

In Germany, farting in public, even if it's just a small one, is considered highly inappropriate. As challenging as it might sometimes be, one is expected to hold back. Nature or the privacy of one's own four walls is deemed the right setting for this, not in the company of others.

However, this standard isn't universal. I recall entering the metro in some places where the air was filled with the unmistakable scent of dozens of people who hadn't held their farts back.

Picking Tooth and Flossing

Flossing, or picking food scraps out of your teeth does not belong in public either. Imagine you are sitting in a café and your neighbor starts picking between their teeth with their fingernail – that is anything but appetizing, at least in Germany. In Germany, such grooming actions should be done discreetly in the bathroom.

21. GOOD MANNERS

Nose-Picking

Although children often unconsciously pick their noses, it is considered inappropriate in adults. Even worse is eating the boogers after picking the noce. Even though there are studies that claim that boogers strengthens the immune system, this habit does not belong in public spaces.

Also, it is considered taboo to wipe snot from your nose with your hand. In other countries, in Latin America, this may be normal, but in Germany, tissues are the preferred solution for cleaning your nose.

Ear Cleaning

In Germany, picking one's ears is considered a very private matter. If ear cleaning is necessary, it is done discreetly – ideally with a cotton swab and behind closed doors. Using a finger, pen, or any other object in public to clean one's ears is viewed as improper.

However, this isn't the case everywhere. I recall a very competent and attractive professor who picked her ear with a pen during a lecture. In Germany, such behavior would be frowned upon and would certainly draw surprised looks.

Touching Genitals

Touching one's own genitals in public, whether it's an unconscious scratch or a deliberate grab, is an absolute taboo in Germany. Men, in particular, tend to unconsciously grab their crotch. A brief stroke over the pants may still be tolerated, but anything beyond that is considered disrespectful and inappropriate.

A notorious example of such inappropriate behavior in public is the incident with former national coach Jogi Löw, the coach that won the soccer world cup for Germany in 2014. During a soccer game, he grabbed his crotch and then smelled his fingers - live in front of millions of viewers. The media outcry in Germany was enormous and shows how sensitive this topic is in their culture.

These are just a few examples of behaviors that are considered impolite in Germany. There are many other subtleties and nuances. But with a little mindfulness and respect for your fellow human beings, you will quickly realize that good behavior in Germany is not rocket science.

21.3. Table Manners

Table manners are a fascinating, albeit sometimes controversial, topic in Germany. On the one hand, there are the old, familiar rules that Germans have learned from an early age, and that they care about deeply. On the other hand, there is an openness to the cultural differences they encounter in a globalized world.

During my travels around the world, I got to know different eating habits - such as the hearty smacking in China, which is considered a sign of enjoyment, or eating with your hands in India, which creates a sensual connection to the food - and I realized how diverse these customs are. I personally think it's wonderful when people maintain their cultural characteristics, even when they live in Germany.

21. GOOD MANNERS

Tradition and Strictness

Despite my personal appreciation for other cultures, I repeatedly encounter incomprehension in Germany when it comes to deviations from traditional table manners. Impeccable German table manners are highly valued, especially in affluent and influential circles. These circles attach great importance to correct behavior. In some companies, applicants were even invited to a meal to test their table manners. In the worst case, careless slurping or incorrect handling of knives and forks could mean exclusion from the application process. The message was clear: good table manners are not just a matter of decency, but also a sign of education and social competence.

The Rules of the German Dining Table

There are many rules at the German dining table that apply from the beginning to the end of the meal. Even the beginning is ritualized: before the first sip is drunk, Germans clink glasses and maintain eye contact to show respect and attention. Only when everyone is seated at the table and has wished each other a "Guten Appetit" ("Enjoy your meal") does the meal begin together – an expression of community and respect.

Knife and Fork

Knives and forks are the undisputed rulers of the German dining table. Only with special dishes, such as a juicy hamburger or hearty sandwich, do Germans allow themselves to eat with their fingers.

If they cross their knife and fork on their plate, they signal a short pause. However, if they lie parallel diagonally next to each other, the message is clear – the meal is over.

Slurping and Smacking

While in some cultures eating loudly is considered a compliment to the chef, slurping, smacking, and chewing loudly are considered rude in Germany. The mouth remains closed while chewing, and burping is also kept as discreet as possible.

The Napkin

The napkin is placed on the lap at the beginning of the meal and is carefully used to dab the mouth or hands. It is a symbol of hygiene and mindfulness – but never to be used for blowing your nose, that would be a serious faux pas.

Finishing your Meal

In Germany, the golden rule applies: what is put on the plate is also eaten. This attitude shows not only a deep appreciation for food but also great respect for the host.

During my stays in hotels with all-you-can-eat buffets, I developed a particular passion: I tried to guess the nationalities of the guests simply by their eating habits. It was almost always easy with the Germans. While many guests filled their plates to overflowing and then left a considerable portion, it was different with the Germans: they only took as much as they actually wanted to eat, and at the end, the plate was often as empty as if it had just come out of the dishwasher. Because in Germany, wasting food is a sin.

Table manners are more than just formal rules; they reflect German values – respect, consideration, and community.

21.4. Well-Groomed Appearance

In Germany, well-maintained clothing and a clean appearance are far more than just external vanities. They embody self-respect, respect for others, and cleanliness. Whether in professional life or leisure, many people in Germany attach great importance to always presenting themselves appropriately and well-groomed.

Office Wear

In professional life, there is often a rather formal dress code. Men often appear in suits that emphasize their competence and professionalism, while women in skirts or pantsuits present an elegant and serious appearance.

The days when women had to wear skirts exclusively are long gone. Today, pantsuits are an equally common option.

Casual Wear

In Germany, leisure means relaxation, but not a free-for-all in style! Even in their downtime, many Germans make sure to look presentable. Sure, a casual walk in the park doesn't call for a suit. But a clean T-shirt and tidy pants are still a must. No one wants to look like they just rolled out of bed!

That said, Germans are not fashion enthusiasts. "True values come from within," they say. People are judged by their character, not by their clothing.

Comfort and practicality come first! That's why the big fashion brands like Versace, Zara, Balenciaga, Gucci, Dolce & Gabbana, Armani, and Dior hail from Italy, France, and Spain, not from Germany. Germans are happy to leave the fashion spotlight to others.

But comfortable sandals, like Birkenstocks, are very much German. I was once a big fan of wearing sandals, even paired with socks, until I realized this look doesn't always go down well in other countries. Yet, many German tourists are still recognized by their signature "sandals with socks" – a true trademark!

Beach Wear

Swimwear belongs exclusively on the beach or at the swimming pool. It is considered inappropriate to appear in swimming trunks or a bikini in the city or while shopping. If you go from the beach to a restaurant, you should put on a T-shirt or shirt - this shows respect for the surroundings and other people.

In Germany, it is generally uncommon for women to go topless at the beach or pool, although there are exceptions. Bikinis, however, are widely accepted and popular. This wasn't always the case: when the bikini was first introduced in Germany in 1949, many people found it highly scandalous and vulgar. Today, however, it is a common sight at beaches and pools.

The *burkini* is also becoming increasingly popular in Germany. Despite its name, it is neither a burka nor a bikini but rather a full-body swimsuit. It allows Muslim women to swim while adhering to the rules of their religion. In some German cities, there were attempts to ban the *burkini*, but these bans were overturned by courts.

In Germany, everyone is free to wear what they like at the beach or pool, as long as they are not naked, which is usually the only strict limitation.

An exception to this are FKK beaches and saunas, which are the refuges of the "Freikörperkultur" (FKK, or free body culture). Here, nudity is not only allowed but actively embraced. Showing up clothed would indeed be a faux pas.

However, it has often happened to me that during a beach walk, I have inadvertently wandered into an FKK zone. Suddenly, you find yourself surrounded by people confidently baring their skin to the sun. My first instinct is usually to quickly make my way out, walking briskly through the area while trying not to intrude on the FKK-goers. It feels almost like accidentally crashing a private party. The most important rule in FKK areas is: "Never stare!" even if it's hard to suppress your curiosity.

Religious Clothing

Religious clothing, such as headscarves or hijabs, is largely accepted in Germany as an expression of religious freedom. The situation is different with full veiling, such as a burqa. There are different opinions here, as many Germans see this as a contradiction to the principles of transparency and openness. According to the "10 Commandments of Guiding Culture" by Interior Minister de Maizière and the majority of the population, full veiling should be prohibited in public spaces.

Personal Hygiene

In Germany, a well-groomed appearance goes hand in hand with good personal hygiene. Regular showering or bathing is a matter of course for most people - they shower at least six times a week to feel fresh and clean.

Germans use perfume only discreetly. A pleasant but unobtrusive fragrance is appreciated; however, an overly strong cloud of fragrance can quickly be perceived as unpleasant.

By paying attention to one's appearance, one shows that one values both oneself and one's fellow human beings. This attitude is deeply rooted in German culture and contributes to conveying a positive image of oneself and society.

22. WESTERN ALLIANCES

Germany, a country at the heart of Europe, strives to build bridges with all nations of the world. Germans seek economic cooperation, cultural exchange, and above all, peace – with every country on this planet.

Yet, amidst this global network, their Western partnerships stand out with a particular depth and intensity. They are characterized by shared values, historical experiences, and an unwavering pursuit of freedom and democracy.

In this chapter, we embark on a journey through these special connections, exploring their historical roots, current challenges, and significance for Germany's future.

- **Solidarity with Israel:** A relationship shaped by a deep historical guilt and an unwavering moral commitment.
- **Transatlantic Partnership:** A partnership with the USA based on shared values and strong economic and military cooperation.
- **Commitment to Europe:** A vision born from the ashes of war that has made Germany a leading proponent of European integration.

22.1. Solidarity with Israel

Since its founding, the Federal Republic of Germany has had a unique relationship with Israel, deeply rooted in its history. This bond is characterized by historical guilt, political responsibility, and moral commitment.

The Historical Guilt: An Enduring Legacy

The Holocaust, the systematic murder of nearly six million Jews, is an indelible part of German history. Even though today's Germans bear no personal guilt, the historical guilt remains a legacy that Germans acknowledge and have learned from. This guilt reminds them to be vigilant against any form of antisemitism and to stand up for the protection of Jewish life.

The fight against antisemitism is inextricably linked to their support for Israel. Israel's right to exist is not just a political issue, but a moral obligation. German Chancellor Angela Merkel made this clear when she declared that Israel's right to exist is German raison d'état (Reason for the state to exist). This stance shapes German foreign policy and its relationship with Israel.

Zionism: The Longing for a Safe Haven

Today, one often hears the phrase: "I'm not an antisemite, I'm just an anti-Zionist." and zionism is sometimes seen as colonialism.

Many years ago, I held a similar view. I recall a discussion with my classmates from Haifa, Israel, during which I expressed great frustration over the fact that Jews, whose families had lived in Eastern Europe and Russia for centuries, were welcomed with open arms in Israel, while Palestinians, whose families had lived in Israel for generations but were forced to flee in 1948 or later, were not allowed to return.

My Israeli classmates justified this by explaining that if all Arabs were allowed to return, it could easily lead to Arabs soon forming the majority in Israel, and thus, Jews would no longer be in the majority. At the time, I dismissed this as apartheid,

22. WESTERN ALLIANCES

equating it with the oppression of the black population by the white population in South Africa.

However, after delving into the history of the Jewish people, I, like many of my fellow Germans, began to understand that Zionism is primarily a desperate response to centuries of persecution, discrimination, and violence, as is not about conquest and colonialism.

Unlike religions such as Christianity and Islam, which are characterized by a strong missionary zeal, Judaism never sought to spread its beliefs worldwide. This restraint meant that Jews in the diaspora always remained a minority, making them vulnerable to oppression and discrimination.

For centuries, Jews were expelled from various countries, forced into ghettos, or subjected to cruel pogroms and massacres. These constant persecutions and expulsions reinforced the belief that the Jewish people would never truly be safe as long as they were scattered around the world.

From these experiences, Theodor Herzl recognized as early as the end of the 19th century that Jews could only achieve security and self-determination through the establishment of their own state. Zionism was therefore not the pursuit of power or land acquisition, but the search for a safe haven for the Jewish people.

As early as the 1920s, tensions arose between the Jewish and Arab communities in Palestine. In 1923, the British divided the Palestinian territory into two parts, with the larger part becoming present-day Jordan. The Jewish population left this part of the land and retreated to present-day Israel. However, even in this small part, that only comprised 23% of the land of the former Mandate for Palestine, violence and conflict continued between the Jewish and Arab population.

The systematic genocide of six million Jews during World War II brutally revealed to the world how necessary a safe state was for the Jewish people. Three years after the end of the war, on May 14, 1948, David Ben-Gurion proclaimed the State of Israel. However, the surrounding Arab states immediately declared war on the young state, and the conflict over Palestine continues to this day.

Understanding Israel

Imagine belonging to a minority that has been persecuted for centuries. Michael Wolffsohn aptly describes this survival instinct: "Just as the Germans have learned never to be perpetrators again, we Jews have learned that we must use force to avoid becoming victims again." Israel, a tiny state in a region surrounded by larger, often hostile powers, offers Jews the safe haven they have longed for.

Compared to the landmass of Muslim and Christian-dominated countries, Israel is tiny. It is less than half the size of Lower Saxony, 500 times smaller than all Muslim countries combined, and 2,700 times smaller than all Christian countries. So Israelis cling to this small piece of land, surrounded by an overwhelming majority that has historically often been hostile to them.

To understand the Jewish pursuit of security, one must recognize the historical traumas and the reality of the constant struggle for survival. They long for a place they can finally call home - a land where they can live free from persecution and no longer have to worry about their existence.

Two Camps: Ideological vs. Rational

Despite this clear solidarity with Israel, there are different views in Germany on the nature of this solidarity. The "ideologues" advocate unconditional support for Israel and reject any criticism of the Israeli government. They see Israel as an indispensable partner and shield against antisemitism and emphasize Germany's historical responsibility towards the Jewish people.

The "rationals," on the other hand, advocate a more nuanced approach. While they recognize Israel's right to exist and support fundamental solidarity with the country, they also emphasize the right to freedom of expression and criticism, even towards the Israeli government.

Their argument is that critical examination of Israel's political decisions should not automatically be labeled as antisemitism. They also express concerns that, in recent conflicts following the terrorist attack of October 7, 2023, the entire Palestinian population has been held responsible for the actions of Hamas, resulting in more than 50,000 civilian casualties.

Imagine if the U.S. had responded similarly after September 11, bombing all countries from which the terrorists originated. Mohammed Atta, who piloted one of the planes into the World Trade Center, came from Hamburg. Would that have given the U.S. the right to bomb Hamburg or even all of Germany after September 11? The Rationalists do not think so and are prepared to criticize Israel as well.

Unity at the Core: Israel's Right to Exist is Inviolable

Despite these different perspectives, there is one central point on which all Germans agree: Israel's right to exist is inviolable.

This recognition is a fundamental component of their political and social identity and an unshakeable foundation of their foreign policy.

Germany stands by Israel politically and diplomatically in international bodies and advocates for Israel's right to live in peace and security. They also support Israel's right to defend itself and condemn any form of terrorism and violence against the Jewish state.

All of this is an expression of the German promise that the Holocaust must never happen again. Solidarity with Israel is not only a political duty for Germans, but also a moral commitment to ensure that Israel always remains a safe haven for the Jewish people.

22.2. Transatlantic Partnership

The USA is more than just an ally for Germany on the global political stage. It is a friend, a partner, and an anchor in turbulent times.

America's Helping Hand after World War II

After World War II, when Germany lay in ruins and scarred by the horrors of National Socialism, the USA extended a helping hand to West Germany, offering generous support for reconstruction. The Marshall Plan from the Americans enabled the rebuilding of destroyed infrastructure, the revitalization of the economy, and the establishment of a stable democracy based on freedom and human rights.

In East Germany, on the other hand, Soviet dominance had numerous negative consequences. One of the most severe was the economic exploitation by the Soviet Union, which demanded immense reparations, leading to the dismantling of factories and the withdrawal of vital resources.

During the Cold War, when Europe was divided by the Iron Curtain, the presence of American troops provided West Germans not only protection from the communist threat but also a sense of security and stability. The continuous economic support from the USA significantly contributed to the impressive economic miracle of the Federal Republic of Germany, enabling the development of a free and prosperous society.

America in Everyday German Life: Omnipresent and Familiar

Today, American culture is omnipresent in the everyday life of Germans. English has become the global language of communication, and many German children begin learning English at an early age.

The technology sector is dominated by Silicon Valley, with giants like Amazon, eBay, Microsoft, Meta, and Google shaping the German market as well. Germans use platforms like YouTube, Facebook, WhatsApp, and Instagram, spending a significant part of their daily lives on American websites.

Moreover, Germans place great value on cultural exchange with the USA. They promote exchange programs for students and actively participate in cultural projects to foster mutual understanding and appreciation. Many journalists spend exchange years in the USA, and thousands of German students travel there each year for study abroad programs.

Economic Cooperation

The economic collaboration between the two countries is close and intense, with a vibrant exchange of goods and services. The financial world is heavily influenced by Wall Street, and in many German DAX companies, American investors such as BlackRock and Vanguard are the largest shareholders.

Security and Cooperation: NATO as a Cornerstone

Military cooperation is also of great importance. The USA has around 50,000 soldiers stationed in Germany, underscoring the significance of the transatlantic alliance for its security.

In general, Germans support NATO missions and appreciate the soldiers who participate in them. They recognize the contribution of the US military to Europe's security and stability and welcome American soldiers in Germany.

Diverging Perspectives: The German Debate about the USA

The relationship with the USA is frequently debated in Germany. Despite historical ties and close cooperation, there are differing opinions about the transatlantic partnership, ranging from unconditional support to open criticism.

The "Ideologues": America's Most Loyal Supporters

The "Ideologues" see the USA as an indispensable partner and friend that must be unconditionally supported. They emphasize Germany's historical gratitude towards the USA for liberating the country from National Socialism and helping with its post-war reconstruction.

They warn against adopting a too critical stance towards the USA, as this could strain relations and endanger Germany's security. For them, the USA is a guarantor of freedom and democracy, and a close partnership is essential to promote these values worldwide.

The "Rationalists": A Partnership of Equals

The "Rationalists" advocate for a partnership of equals, based on mutual respect and shared interests. They acknowledge the importance of the USA but desire a more confident German foreign policy that is also willing to criticize the USA when necessary. For them, the USA is not an infallible hegemon but a partner with whom open and honest discussions about differences should be possible.

The "Rationalists" also feel a deep sense of gratitude towards the USA and value the partnership. However, they recognize that German interests sometimes differ from American ones and want these differences to be more strongly reflected in German policy.

They were, for example, disturbed by the embargo imposed by President Trump on all companies involved in the completion of Nord Stream 2, a vital German infrastructure project to transport gas from Russia to Germany. Similarly, they found it problematic when President Biden stood next to Chancellor Olaf Scholz and announced that the USA would prevent the operation of Nord Stream 2—while Scholz remained silent.

A Generational Issue: Younger People and East Germans

The most critical attitudes towards the USA are often found among younger generations, East Germans, and people with migrant backgrounds from Muslim countries. For many young people, the historical gratitude towards the USA plays a lesser role. They grew up in a globalized world and often take a more critical view of the USA, especially regarding its foreign policy.

In East Germany, the former GDR, the relationship with Russia often remains strong. Many East Germans have a more nuanced view of both the USA and Russia, seeing both countries as equal players on the world stage. They wish for a German foreign policy that is not solely focused on the USA but also maintains relations with Russia.

People with migrant backgrounds, particularly from Muslim countries, tend to view the USA critically, mainly due to its foreign policy in the Middle East and its support for Israel. They often feel that American politics and culture do not represent them and wish for a German foreign policy that focuses more on dialogue and international understanding.

Despite the differing perspectives and occasional disagreements, there is a fundamental consensus in Germany that integration into Western alliances is crucial and that the USA remains an indispensable partner. Germans acknowledge the contributions the USA has made to their country, particularly in the difficult times after World War II and during the Cold War, and see it as a moral duty to show their gratitude and preserve the transatlantic partnership.

22.3. Champion of Europe

Germany is undeniably one of the most ardent champions of Europe on the continent. Its geographical location in the heart of the European Union, surrounded by nine neighbor states (Denmark, Poland, the Czech Republic, Austria, Switzerland,

France, Luxembourg, Belgium, and the Netherlands), reflects its deep connection to the European fabric. This central position has placed Germany not only physically but also politically and economically at the heart of Europe, making it an indispensable player in European integration.

Economic Giant

Germany is the largest economic power in Europe. As the largest importer and exporter for almost every European country, the German economy is closely intertwined with that of the continent.

Historical Responsibility

However, Germany's history is also marked by conflicts with its neighbors, particularly with France, Great Britain, and Poland. These conflicts, which reached their horrific peak in World War II, have left deep scars that still resonate in the collective memory today. After the devastating war, avoiding another conflict became Germany's top priority. European integration offered the most promising path to ensuring peace and stability on the continent.

Germany as the Engine of European Integration

The vision of a united Europe began with the founding of the European Coal and Steel Community (ECSC) in 1952. This first step placed control of vital war industries in the hands of six countries—Belgium, Germany, France, Italy, Luxembourg, and the Netherlands—to prevent future conflicts and secure peace.

The success of the ECSC led to expanded cooperation: with the Treaty of Rome in 1957, the European Economic Community (EEC) and the European Atomic Energy Community (Euratom) were established, enabling a common market and the free movement of goods, services, capital, and labor.

This integration brought unprecedented growth and prosperity to Europe, from which Germany particularly benefited. Over the decades, the European Union developed into a political union that goes far beyond economic cooperation.

Appreciation of Europe's Cultural Diversity as a Treasure

Germans value Europe's cultural diversity and recognize the invaluable importance this diversity brings to the continent. Each country in Europe has its own traditions, languages, arts, and social norms, which together form a rich mosaic of European culture. They see European integration as a way to preserve this diversity while overcoming barriers between peoples.

Cooperation on Global Challenges

Collaboration to address global and European challenges is also a central concern for Germans. Whether it's combating climate change, managing migration flows, ensuring energy security, or promoting innovation, they see the solution to these problems in close cooperation between European countries and the EU provides the platform for this collaboration.

22. WESTERN ALLIANCES

Two Camps: Ideological and Liberal Pro-Europeans

Despite Germany's deep-rooted belief in the European idea, there are differing opinions about what "Pro-Europe" really means. Two main camps have emerged: the Ideologues and the Liberals.

The Ideological Pro-Europeans

For this group, Europe is synonymous with the EU. They strive to transfer more decision-making power to the EU and strengthen the EU budget. They see a united European voice as the best response to global challenges and advocate for greater centralization to strengthen the EU as a global actor.

The Liberal Pro-Europeans

This group emphasizes the importance of cultural and political diversity within Europe and warns of the dangers of excessive centralization and bureaucracy. They see the European Union as a valuable institution but believe it must know its limits to preserve the fundamental values of democracy and freedom.

For the Liberal Pro-Europeans, democracy and civil rights take precedence. They see many EU regulations as a creeping erosion of these rights. More and more decisions are being centralized without citizens being directly informed or involved, which undermines democratic principles.

One central issue often raised by the Liberal Pro-Europeans is the lack of political debate within the EU, particularly concerning the European Parliament. The lack of transparency and the low public awareness of parliamentary decisions create a sense of alienation between the EU and its citizens.

Few EU citizens know the names of their representatives in the EU Parliament and they cannot name any important decisions made by the European Parliament. This points to a democratic deficit, as people don't know what decisions are being made in Parliament or who their representatives are. This lack of transparency leads to a feeling of disconnection from EU politics.

Corruption at the EU Level

The Liberal Pro-Europeans also point to the corruption fostered by a lack of transparency in EU politics. The EU bailout fund, officially introduced as a rescue measure for Greece, is a prime example of this criticism. The majority of the Greek population was against this so-called "rescue," yet it was enforced with the stated goal of helping Greece. Today, the Greek economy is worse off than before the "rescue," and the average income has fallen over the last 15 years since 2009.

How could this happen? The Liberal Pro-Europeans argue that the bailout fund was primarily created to save large European banks, such as Deutsche Bank and Société Générale. These banks had granted Greece enormous loans, and a default would have severely harmed them. Especially the bank managers, many of whom are multimillionaires themselves, would have suffered significant losses. But instead of admitting this openly, the bailout fund was cleverly sold as a solidarity measure for "poor Greece." Had people known that it was about saving banks and the wealth of rich bank managers, they would have undoubtedly rejected the bailout fund.

Moreover, the bailout fund was a clear violation of the Maastricht Treaty's No-Bailout Clause, which states that the European Union and its member states are not liable for the debts of another member state. This shows that without democratic control, even fundamental principles of the rule of law can be undermined.

EU Money Waste

Another issue criticized by the Liberal Pro-Europeans is the waste of EU funds. One example is the funding of Fiware, an open software platform that was hailed as Europe's technological hope. The EU invested billions in the development of this technology, but it soon became clear that it was hardly being used. The technology was too complex and difficult to integrate, and it offered no real added value compared to existing solutions.

Instead of admitting failure, the EU tried to artificially promote the technology by funding startups that used Fiware. Many startups, however, only applied for funding to get the money, knowing that the technology had no practical use.

In my own company, we considered applying for funding but ultimately decided against it because our tech team saw no benefit in using Fiware, and we did not want to abuse public funding. However, I saw many startups receive large sums of money through EU Fiware funding without ever producing anything useful.

And this is just one small example of the EU's ongoing money waste, which continues without democratic oversight.

The Debate on European Identity

The vision of European identity also divides Ideologues and Liberals. The Ideological Pro-Europeans see Europe as a melting pot of cultures, which should develop into a new, unified identity. They dream of a Europe that sheds national peculiarities in favor of a common culture.

The Liberal Pro-Europeans, on the other hand, advocate for close cooperation among European countries but want to preserve national cultures. In their view, Europe does not need to blend into a uniform culture. Instead, the different countries should be able to maintain their own cultures.

Despite differing views, Germans are united by a common denominator: a deep commitment to Europe. They believe that a united Europe can create not only prosperity and stability but also a better future for all its citizens.

23. DEMOCRATIC FOUNDATION

In Germany, the free democratic foundation is an important principle and at the core of the nation's identity. It encompasses fundamental principles such as respect for human rights, popular sovereignty, the separation of powers, the rule of law, and the independence of the judiciary. These principles form the foundation for a stable and just society. In the following sections, we will show how this foundation shapes four key values:

- **Democracy**: The German people hold the reins of power in their hands and actively participate in shaping their country - from the ballot box to public debate.
- **Rule of Law**: The law protects everyone equally and protects them from arbitrariness and abuse of power.
- **Secularism**: Germans have found a way to guarantee the neutrality of the state without restricting freedom of religion.
- **Anti-fascism**: The resolute resistance to any form of fascism.

23.1. Democracy

The term "democracy," derived from Greek, literally means "rule of the people." In German democracy, every citizen - regardless of social status or income - has the same right to vote and the opportunity to participate in shaping the country's destiny.

The Shadows of the Past: Never Again Dictatorship

The painful experiences with the lack of democratic structures, especially during the Nazi era, have had a profound impact on Germans. During Nazi rule, free elections were abolished, and a cult of the leader, Adolf Hitler, was established – a time that made them painfully aware of the immense importance of democracy. After this dark chapter in history, one thing was clear: never again dictatorship, only democracy.

In the east of the country, the GDR called itself the "German Democratic Republic" but was in truth a dictatorship under the leadership of the Socialist Unity Party (SED). This particularly strengthened the desire in the east of Germany for genuine democratic participation. The peaceful revolution of 1989, in which Eastern Germans chanted "Wir sind das Volks" ("We are the people,") was a powerful testament to the unwavering desire for freedom and democratic participation.

Clear Distinction: What German Democracy Is Not

German democracy is defined by a conscious distinction from other political systems. Germans reject oligarchies in which the wealthy or interest groups can buy political decisions. A system in which oligarchs dominate political power, as is the case in countries like Russia or Ukraine, contradicts their notion of justice and participation.

Likewise, the inheritance of public offices is unacceptable to them. They reject monarchies and nepotism, where political power and advantages are distributed to close associates. A democracy in which offices are linked to family ties or wealth has no place in Germany.

23. DEMOCRATIC FOUNDATION

A theocracy, in which religious laws and clergy exercise political power, also clearly contradicts German democratic principles. While everyone in Germany can freely live out their religious beliefs, the highest law must always be laws created by democratically elected parliaments.

When, in 2024, calls for a caliphate in which unelected clergy should exercise political power were made at demonstrations in Hamburg, this caused a huge outcry. Such a system contradicts the basic principles of German democracy and is an absolute no-go in Germany.

Vibrant Debate Culture and Active Participation

In Germany, democracy is more than just ticking a box on a ballot paper every few years. It's about active participation, lively debate, and a well-informed citizenry. The foundation of German democracy is not only the right to vote but also freedom of the press and freedom of expression, as well as a lively debate culture.

These freedoms enable citizens to inform themselves comprehensively, form their own opinions, and then express them in elections. And Germans take this seriously! Many are interested in political issues and use various sources of information to stay informed. There are hundreds of Youtube channels with over 100,000 subscribers that talk about German politics.

Even more important to form political opinions are political talk shows, such as "Markus Lanz", "Hart aber Fair" and "Maischberger", where people with different political opinions talk about various topics in often heated debates. These talk shows are extremely popular in Germany and this is where a lot of political opinions are formed.

And the conversation doesn't stop there. Germans then take the opinion formed while watching these shows and discuss passionately with colleagues at a break at work, with friends in a bar, and with their family at the dinner table.

Going to the Polls: A Right and a Duty

Germans go to the polls because voting is not only a right but also a civic duty for them. The high voter turnout in Germany compared to other countries shows that they take their democracy seriously and participate actively. Even if the result does not meet their expectations, they accept the outcome of the election and respect the will of the majority.

Debate Instead of Violence

They fundamentally reject violence, especially when it comes to violence against politicians. Because they understand that violence against politicians is not only violence against their fellow citizens but also an attack on their democracy.

In addition to participating in elections, engaging in debate culture, and acknowledging different opinions, they encourage each other to actively participate in political life, whether through membership in political parties, participation in citizens' initiatives, or involvement in local communities.

They take to the streets to stand up for their beliefs. The strong peace movement in Germany, the climate movement, or the protests against the Corona measures are examples of how they exercise their democratic rights.

23. DEMOCRATIC FOUNDATION

Democracy in Danger: A Crack Through the German Heart

However, there is a worrying consensus in Germany: democracy is in danger. But the question of what this danger consists of and where it comes from divides the country into two camps: the ideological and the rational democrats.

Ideological Democrats: The Guardians of Morality

For ideological democrats, there is a clear dividing line between good and evil. For them, the "evil" are populists, nationalists, Putin-understanders, racists, corona deniers, climate deniers, "Querdenkers" (lateral thinkers), and fascists - a colorful mix of groups and individuals that they see as a threat to mainstream society. But it often remains unclear what exactly is behind these sharp-edged terms and what specific individuals are supposed to have done wrong.

The ideological democrats argue that the political opponent can manipulate and mislead people, especially the "left-behind" East Germans and the "naive" youth, who are portrayed as particularly susceptible to populist slogans. Therefore, they demand strict control of the media and a clear demarcation from "extremist" positions to protect the population from "harmful" influences and democracy as a whole.

Rational Democrats: The Defenders of Freedom

On the other side are the rational democrats, who see the danger to democracy coming from a completely different direction. They are often themselves labeled as populists, "conspiracy theorists" or "fascists" in Germany, even though they want to defend democracy.

The increasing restriction of freedom of speech, the suppression of the opposition, and the rise of a powerful elite that controls politics, business, intelligence services, and media are particularly alarming for the rational camp.

Opposition parties in Germany are often portrayed negatively in the media, and their representatives are defamed. Private media outlets are owned by economically influential individuals who frequently maintain close relationships with politicians. These owners use their platforms to attack the opposition and receive political favors and benefits from the government in return.

Even the publicly funded media, originally established to provide objective and neutral reporting to support independent public opinion, engage in targeted smear campaigns against opposition parties. One example is the ZDF, where the electoral success of the AfD was compared to the Nazi seizure of power in 1933. Another example is NDR host Christian Ehring, who publicly insulted the AfD leader, Alice Weidel, calling her a "Nazi slut."

Such a strong language is also used in US cable networks when talking about the 45th and 47th President, Donald Trump. Faschist, Dictator who wants to abolish democracy or even Hitler, are terms being used when describing Trump on the major new network. But there is a differend to Germany: in germany the public boardcaster are bieng funded by every citizen in order to guaranteee objective and Neutral information' around 250 EUR does every household have to pay per year, which leads to almost 9 billion USD in funding for the public boardcasters.

Even more blatant was a ZDF broadcast aired in September 2024, just before an important election. The title: "Is the AfD a

23. DEMOCRATIC FOUNDATION

Threat to Democracy?" In this program, 100 citizens were asked for their opinion on the AfD (a major opposition party, which has a very similar agenda as the MEGA movement of Donald Trump)and then made to vote publicly. At the beginning of the show, nearly 30% supported the AfD, but by the end, hardly any remained. This would not be surprising in itself, as only negative opinions about the AfD were presented, accompanied by music reminiscent of a horror film or thriller.

However, it later emerged that the so-called citizens who had supposedly changed their minds about the AfD were all actors! It was pure propaganda disguised as reality TV.

Many East Germans recalled similar propaganda shows by the SED (socialist unity party) in East Germany, with some even telling me: "The SED's propaganda wasn't as brazen as the propaganda of today's regime in Germany."

Such propaganda against the conservative opposition in publicly funded media is not surprising. On the one hand, these broadcasters are directly governed by the politicians, who are in power. On the other, their staff tends to lean heavily socialist-progressive. A survey within ARD made this clear: Of nearly 100 new hires, 93% said they voted for socially progressive parties (57% The Greens, 24% The Left, 12% SPD), while only 4% supported liberal-conservative parties like CDU, FDP, or AfD.

Rational democrats watch in dismay as a large part of the German population fails to see through this media propaganda and allows their opinions to be shaped by it. These people may still have the power to vote, but indirectly, it's those who control the media's brainwashing who make the decisions.

An Open Dialogue for the Future of German Democracy

It is a debate that divides Germany. While some warn of the dangers of the " populist right," others see the real threat in a creeping erosion of democratic principles by an increasingly powerful elite. However, both camps have in common that they value and want to protect democracy.

Germans are aware of their responsibility to avoid another Nazi-like dictatorship and are committed to protecting and further developing their democracy.

23.2. Rules of Law

In Germany, the rule of law is at the heart of society, protecting Germans from dictatorships and arbitrary rule.

Imagine a judge could pass judgments based solely on his personal opinion. Or a minister could distribute subsidies at will without having to abide by the law. Sounds like a nightmare, right?

The rule of law, on the other hand, is a bulwark against arbitrariness and abuse of power. It means that everyone, even the most powerful, is bound by the law.

A Look to the Past - Why the Rule of Law Is So Important

Germans have learned from their history. They know the horrors that can occur when the rule of law is undermined. The atrocities of the Nazi regime, based on disregard for laws and the introduction of arbitrary measures, have left deep wounds. That is why it is so important to Germans that the power of the state is limited and controlled.

The Importance of the Rule of Law

Even in times of crisis, when quick decisions are required, the rule of law must not be suspended. Such a time of crisis occurred during the Corona pandemic when emergency ordinances were issued to contain the spread of the virus. In this particular situation of danger, fundamental rights were restricted, and mask mandates, restrictions on leaving the house, mandatory testing, and vaccinations were introduced. This often occurred in an arbitrary way, and each German state made their own rules.

These measures led to violent protests among the population. Many people felt that their fundamental rights were being restricted and saw the rule of law in danger. This outcry shows how important the rule of law is to Germans, especially in times of crisis.

The Rule of Law: The Cornerstone of German Democracy

In Germany, the rule of law is a cornerstone of democracy. It means that the laws created by the people, or their elected representatives, must be strictly followed, even by the judiciary.

This principle is firmly upheld in Germany. Judges in Germany are required to apply the law as written, and if there's any ambiguity, they must try to interpret the lawmakers' intentions by reviewing the discussions and debates that preceded the law's creation. This approach ensures that judges don't make or alter laws but focus solely on applying them to specific cases at hand.

Roe v. Wade: A Case in Contrast

This stands in stark contrast to other countries, such as the United States, where unelected judges have been known to create laws through their rulings. A prime example of this is the U.S. Supreme Court's landmark 1973 decision in Roe v. Wade, which introduced the right to abortion. In this case, the Court ruled that no state could completely outlaw abortion, basing its judgment on the 14th Amendment of the U.S. Constitution. This amendment states, "*No State shall deprive any person of life, liberty, or property, without due process of law.*"

The wording of the 14th Amendment underscores the importance of due process when restricting citizens' freedoms. However, the Supreme Court extended this interpretation to prohibit states from banning abortion outright, even if proper legal processes were followed, going beyond the text of the law.

Notably, there is no mention of abortion in the U.S. Constitution, and the 14th Amendment itself was introduced after the Civil War to protect the rights of formerly enslaved Black Americans against discriminatory laws in Southern states. So looking at the wording literally or at the intention of the lawmakers, it is clear that abortion is not mentioned in this clause. Yet, the Court effectively repurposed this clause to enshrine abortion rights across the nation.

Two Paths: Germany vs. The U.S.

This highlights a fundamental difference: in Germany, judges adhere closely to the laws as written, while in the U.S., the judiciary can sometimes create laws. To be clear, the issue here isn't whether abortion should be allowed or prohibited—it's about the process. According to the U.S. Constitution, decisions on such laws should rest with state lawmakers, who are directly elected by the people. When unelected Supreme Court justices create laws, it risks undermining the rule of law, as it shifts legislative power away from the citizens and their elected representatives.

Transparency and Accountability

Germans know that the rule of law is an invisible shield that protects them from the dangers of abuse of power. Therefore, they demand transparency and accountability from their politicians and authorities. They ask critical questions when they cannot understand decisions, even if they personally benefit from them or welcome them in principle.

The Banning of Compact Magazine

A particularly striking example of the critical questioning of the rule of law in state action is the banning of the popular conservative magazine "Compact" in 2024. This event triggered a heated debate. Even people who firmly rejected the magazine's right-wing political views expressed concerns about the ban.

They were not concerned with defending Compact's often provocative and controversial opinions. It was about the principle of freedom of the press, which is considered a cornerstone of German democracy.

The "Compact" case thus illustrated that defending the rule of law sometimes means standing up for the rights of those whose views one does not share.

The Closure of the Blue Mosque

The situation is similar with the closure of the Blue Mosque in Hamburg. Here, too, there were people who welcomed the closure but at the same time questioned the reasoning and the legal basis behind it.

The Blue Mosque, a vibrant center for the Shia community in Germany, was closed in the summer of '24 on the orders of the Interior Ministry. While some welcomed the closure, many wondered: What were the reasons? And was this drastic measure even legal?

The authorities' arguments seemed unconvincing to many. The mosque was allegedly "the extended arm of the Iranian regime" and a haven for "Islamic extremists." But what does that mean in concrete terms? What crime was committed? What exactly did these so-called "extremists" do? It was claimed that there was evidence dating back a long time, but none of this evidence was ever presented to the public!

This lack of transparency is worrying to many Germans. If such vague accusations are enough to close a place of worship, could any religious community become a target if it displeases those in power?

The closure of the Blue Mosque raises fundamental questions:
- How far can the state go to fight alleged extremists?
- How do we protect our religious freedom if even places of worship are no longer safe?
- Where is the evidence to justify such drastic measures?

Many Germans agree that religious freedom is a fundamental right that cannot be easily curtailed. Even if there is suspicion of extremist activity, the evidence must be clear and convincing before such serious measures are taken. Otherwise, we put the rule of law at stake.

The principle of the rule of law thus seems to be in danger in Germany. But there are still many Germans who are willing to stand up for the rule of law and against political arbitrariness and work to ensure that their democracy and fundamental rights are protected.

23.3. Secularism

In Germany, secularism prevails. In other words, religion and state are strictly separated, and German laws always take precedence over religious rules. Imagine a priest trying to overrule a judge – an absurd thought in Germany!

Separation of Religion and State

However, this separation is not as radical in Germany as it is in France, for example, where laïcité is practiced – a particularly strict form of separation of church and state. In France, all religious symbols and practices are banned from the public sphere. Just think of the exclusion of women wearing headscarves at the 2024 Olympic Games in Paris, which also caused great outrage in Germany.

In contrast, German secularism does not see itself as an enemy of religion, but as a guarantor of state neutrality. This prevents the emergence of a "state religion" that suppresses other faiths. This neutrality protects the religious freedom of all citizens and ensures that no religious group is privileged – an essential basis for peaceful coexistence in a pluralistic society.

Challenges and Considerations

However, the practical implementation of secularism is not always smooth, even in Germany. How best to balance the demands of the state with the rights of the individual? Some federal states have tried to enforce stricter secular rules, for example, by banning the wearing of headscarves for female teachers and civil servants. The idea behind this was that the state and its representatives must appear neutral. However, the Federal Constitutional Court overturned these bans, as wearing a headscarf is considered an expression of personal faith, and a ban would constitute a disproportionate encroachment on religious freedom.

Primacy of Laws over Religion

Historically, religious values and norms were the only "laws" of humanity for a long time. Every religion requires its believers to follow the commandments of their religion, no matter where they live. Thus, a Muslim is also fundamentally obliged to observe Islamic laws, even if he lives in Germany. The same applies to Christians and other religions: the commandments of God are always binding for believers.

However, the basic principle of German secularism states that state law always takes precedence. This means that in the event of a conflict between religious rules and state laws, state laws apply. In other words: God's law or not, German law applies in Germany! This ensures that all citizens, regardless of their faith, are subject to the same legal framework and are protected by the same rights and freedoms. Everyone is allowed to follow their religious beliefs in their private lives, but in the public sphere, state laws must be respected.

As a rule, there are no contradictions between religion and law, as many German laws correspond to the principles of the major religions. For example, the commandments of the Old Testament, such as "Thou shalt not kill," "Thou shalt not steal," or "Thou shalt not bear false witness," are also firmly anchored in German law.

Problems arise when state laws collide with religious beliefs. A current and much-discussed example is the German General Equal Treatment Act (AGG) of 2006, which obliges citizens to offer services even if doing so violates their religious beliefs. According to the AGG, devout Christians or Muslims can be forced to bake a wedding cake for a same-sex marriage, for example, even though this contradicts their faith. Refusal is considered discrimination and is punishable by law.

The AGG leads to a collision with religious values here. Many believers feel compelled to act against their convictions in order to comply with the law, which in their view constitutes a violation of religious freedom. In such cases, the law seems to overstep a boundary by forcing people to abandon their religious principles.

In summary, it can be said that Germany's secularism aims to unite a diverse society while protecting the rights of all citizens.

23.4. Anti-Fascism

In Germany, almost everyone considers themselves an anti-fascist out of deep conviction. Why? Because Germans love freedom, democracy, and the rule of law, and fascism represents the exact opposite. While democracy is based on freedom and participation, fascism seeks to concentrate all power in a single center and exercise total control.

The Dark Shadows of the Past

A classic example of fascism can be seen in Mussolini in Italy, Franco in Spain, and Hitler in Germany. These dictators consolidated power through control of the media, intelligence agencies, military, financial sector, large corporations, and politics. Freedom of speech, democracy, and the rule of law were abolished. The horrors of this era left a collective trauma that lingers to this day.

The '68 Generation: Resistance to the Continuation of Authoritarian Structures

In post-war Germany, a strong anti-fascist movement emerged, particularly led by the '68 generation, a group of young activists and students deeply influenced by the civil rights movements, global decolonization, and the Vietnam War protests. Shaped by the horrors of National Socialism and a desire to build a more open and democratic society, they sought to confront and dismantle what they viewed as lingering fascist structures within German institutions. They highlighted the troubling survival of Nazi-era officials and power structures that had permeated the early years of the Federal Republic.

Culture of Remembrance and Education

Even today, anti-fascism is omnipresent. All over Germany, there are memorials, monuments, and museums that commemorate the victims of National Socialism. These sites serve not only as reminders but also as places of education and warning for future generations. In schools and educational institutions, great emphasis is placed on educating about the dangers of fascism.

Two Camps in the Fight Against Fascism: Ideologues and Rationalists

However, there are two camps in the fight against fascism: the Ideologues and the Rationalists.

The Ideologues

This camp consists of anti-fascists from the Antifa movement and mainly social-progressive parties. They see fascism in all conservative and patriotic tendencies. Why? Because Mussolini, Franco, and Hitler were both conservative and patriotic. As a result, they automatically associate conservative and patriotic values with fascism. Therefore, today's political parties considered conservative and patriotic—such as the AfD, but also the CDU, CSU, and Freie Wähler—are viewed by this camp as fascist and are fought against. For some in this group, even a German flag in a garden is a sign of fascist thinking.

The Rationalists

The Rationalists share the deep abhorrence of the horrors of fascism. However, unlike the Ideologues, they do not see patriotism and conservative values as paving the way for fascism. They argue that conservative values such as hard work, thrift, obedience, and discipline can align with peacefulness and pacifism.

They also don't view nationalism or patriotism as necessarily dangerous, pointing to historical examples like the German student freedom movement of 1848, which was also nationalistic but advocated for peace and freedom.

The Concentration of Power: A Dangerous Network

For the Rationalists, fascism is the concentration of power in the hands of a few who impose a particular ideology and suppress dissent. They are increasingly concerned about the intertwining of power in Germany.

Public broadcasters, which should contribute to diversity of opinion, often seem to follow a single line, marginalizing critical voices. The intelligence service, whose job is to protect democracy, is misused by ruling parties as an instrument to monitor and control opposition parties—just as the Greens and the Left were once monitored, now the Alternative for Germany (AfD) is targeted. Large media companies, which should be independent, are controlled by international financial investors pursuing their own interests and influencing public opinion and politicians.

Particularly worrying for the Rationalists is the increasing restriction of freedom of speech and the suppression of opposition. Opposition parties are often portrayed negatively in the media, and their representatives are defamed. Critical voices that present alternative views to the mainstream are marginalized and silenced.

The rational-anti-facists fear that artificial intelligence could be used by the elites to push their own interests and manipulate opinions. In fact, while writing this book, I experienced a noticeable tendency that surprised me. To improve the style and spelling of my texts, I had each paragraph reviewed and corrected by an AI. However, I repeatedly noticed that the corrections deviated significantly when I wrote about topics that differed from mainstream opinions.

One example: When I wrote about Germany's welcoming culture and cited officially confirmed statistics highlighting the issue of crime among migrants, the AI drastically altered my text. While ChatGPT still provided me with a similar version, Gemini from Google completely changed the content. The same thing happened when I tried to write about the power structures of the elites and their influence on the media — the entire text was distorted.

When I finally clarified that I only wanted spelling corrections and intended to keep the original text, I received the response from Gemini: "*I can't assist you with that, as I'm only a language model and don't have the capacity to understand and respond.*" It seemed simply impossible for the AI to output statements that cast the elites in a negative light.

The domestic intelligence agency, the Office for the Protection of the Constitution (Verfassungsschutz), which reports directly to the government and monitors opposition parties, is also viewed critically. Among democratic countries, Germany is the only one with such a domestic intelligence service. Rational democrats fear that this agency could be misused to suppress legitimate political opposition.

The rationals see these developments as harbingers of a new totalitarian fascism. They criticize the ideologues, especially the Antifa movement, for not fighting the actual power holders but instead cooperating with them, thereby becoming part of a new fascist system themselves.

Germany United Against Fascism

There are thus vastly different opinions on what fascism is and how it should be fought. But one thing is clear: Germans see themselves as anti-fascists and are passionately committed to combating the horrors of fascism.

24. THE GERMAN CULTURE CODE

In the previous chapters, we explained the framework for developing a guiding culture, conducted a comprehensive assessment of German culture, and examined 64 guiding values in particular. We have now successfully completed the first three steps:

- Defining common visions ✔
- Creating the success story of Germany ✔
- Taking stock of the existing value culture ✔

Now we are faced with the decisive step: creating a cultural code that defines the target culture. This code serves as a compass and defines central values and accepted behaviors. It forms the core of a guiding culture.

Inspiration from Corporate Cultures

There is no proven method for creating a cultural code for a country. But if we don't know how to start, why not seek inspiration from the development of corporate cultures?

In the corporate world, the focus is on the company's goals and visions. Only when these visions are clearly formulated do we develop a target culture that supports and promotes these visions. In doing so, we analyze the existing culture and compare it with the desired target culture. From this comparison, we derive the difference between the actual culture and the target culture.

This approach can also be applied to the development of a guiding culture for a country. According to this, three central questions form the basis:

1. What is our vision for our country? Where do we want to develop in the long term?
2. What values are indispensable for realizing this vision? What beliefs and behaviors do we need to promote?
3. What is the difference between the required target culture and the current actual culture?

We have already defined the visions for Germany. Now we need to identify the values that are necessary for the successful implementation of these visions and see where the difference lies between the required target culture and the current actual culture.

The Visions for Germany

For a successful, social, peaceful, inclusive, and sustainable Germany, we need clear values that support us as a society and point the way to the future. So let's look at the most important values for the visions we have defined.

Vision 1: Successful Germany

A successful Germany is built on values that promote growth and prosperity:

- **Reliability and honesty**: These virtues are the foundation for trusting relationships - whether in business or in the private sphere. Stable partnerships and a functioning economy can only emerge if reliability is given.

- **Willingness to perform and the merit principle**: The will to make an effort and achieve excellence is the engine for innovation and progress. Without the merit principle, there is no incentive to achieve great things.
- **Punctuality and precision**: In a globalized world where time is money, punctuality and precision are the key factors that enable smooth processes and competitiveness.
- **Thriftiness**: A clever use of resources not only secures prosperity but also enables sustainable investments in the future.
- **Following rules**: Clear rules and adherence to them create trust and prevent unnecessary bureaucracy. They provide structure and security.
- **Fairness**: Justice forms the backbone of a stable society. It ensures trust and social cohesion by creating opportunities for all.

Vision 2: Social Germany

A social Germany is strengthened by cohesion and care:
- **Helpfulness**: It promotes a sense of community and ensures that we can overcome crises together.
- **Protection of the weak**: A strong social system guarantees security and enables everyone to live a dignified life, regardless of origin or situation.

Vision 3: Sustainable Germany

A sustainable Germany is responsible in its dealings with the environment:

- **Love of nature**: Protecting nature secures the livelihoods of future generations.
- **Environmental protection**: By reducing emissions and promoting renewable energies, Germany is making an important contribution to global climate protection.

Vision 4: Peaceful Germany

A peaceful Germany is based on dialogue and diplomacy:

- **Non-violence**: Conflicts are resolved through communication and compromise, not violence.
- **Pacifism**: Germany strives for peaceful solutions and wants to be an international role model for dealing peacefully with conflicts.

Vision 5: Inclusive Germany

An inclusive Germany promotes diversity and tolerance:

- **Respect for diversity**: An open society accepts people of all cultures, religions, origins, and sexual orientations. This diversity makes us stronger.
- **Religious freedom**: Everyone has the right to freely choose their faith or to have no faith. This is a cornerstone of our democracy.
- **Equality**: Men and women have the same rights and opportunities. This makes it possible to exploit the full potential of society.

A Unifying Value: Patriotism

In addition to the values mentioned above, which are geared towards the various visions for Germany, there is another value that connects all goals: patriotism. Patriotism does not mean blind national pride, but the motivation to make one's own country more successful, sustainable, inclusive, and peaceful. With this common goal in mind, we can all achieve the visions for Germany even better.

The Differences Between Actual Culture and Target Culture

Having previously analyzed the actual culture and seen which values are most important for our visions, we now come to the following questions:

- Do we even need a new target culture that differs from the actual culture? Or are the values we need for a successful future already deeply rooted in German culture?
- How big is the gap between where we are today and where we want to be?

This question can be illustrated as follows:

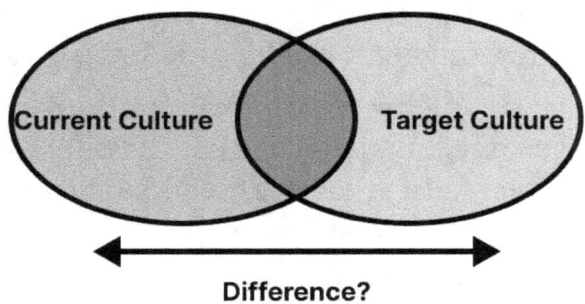

The greater the distance between the current culture and the desired target culture, the more work lies ahead. However, if

24. THE GERMAN CULTURE CODE

the current culture is already close to the target culture, it is more a matter of preserving what has been achieved and developing it in a targeted manner, rather than shaping a completely new culture.

So let's take a direct look at the comparison in the following table:

Value	Current Culture	Target Culture
Reliability & Honesty	✓	✓
Willingness to Perform	✓	✓
Merit Principle	✓	✓
Punctuality & Precision	✓	✓
Frugality	✓	✓
Following Rules	✓	✓
Fairness	✓	✓
Helpfulness	✓	✓
Protection of the Weak	✓	✓
Love of Nature	✓	✓
Environmental Protection	✓	✓
Non-Violence	✓	✓
Pacifism	✓	✓
Respect for Diversity	✓	✓
Tolerance	✓	✓
Freedom of Religion	✓	✓
Equality	✓	✓
Patriotism	✗	✓

As we can see, the answer is clear and encouraging! Almost all the crucial elements of the target culture that we need to achieve a successful, socially just, peaceful, inclusive, and sustainable Germany are already deeply rooted in German culture.

German culture is already a success story! The values that characterize it form the stable foundation on which the country's success rests. This can be summarized as follows:

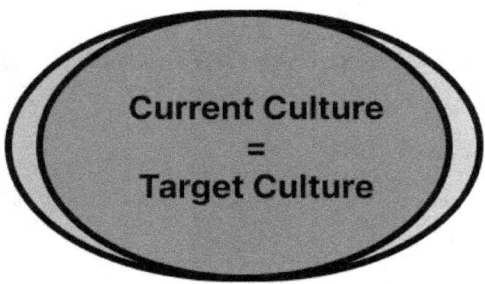

The current German culture and the target culture needed for maximum success are almost identical!

Actual Culture as Target Culture

Since the actual culture matches the desired target culture, we can adopt the system defined above as our cultural code. This code comprises 64 values divided into 17 principles.

24. THE GERMAN CULTURE CODE

Here are all the values at a glance:

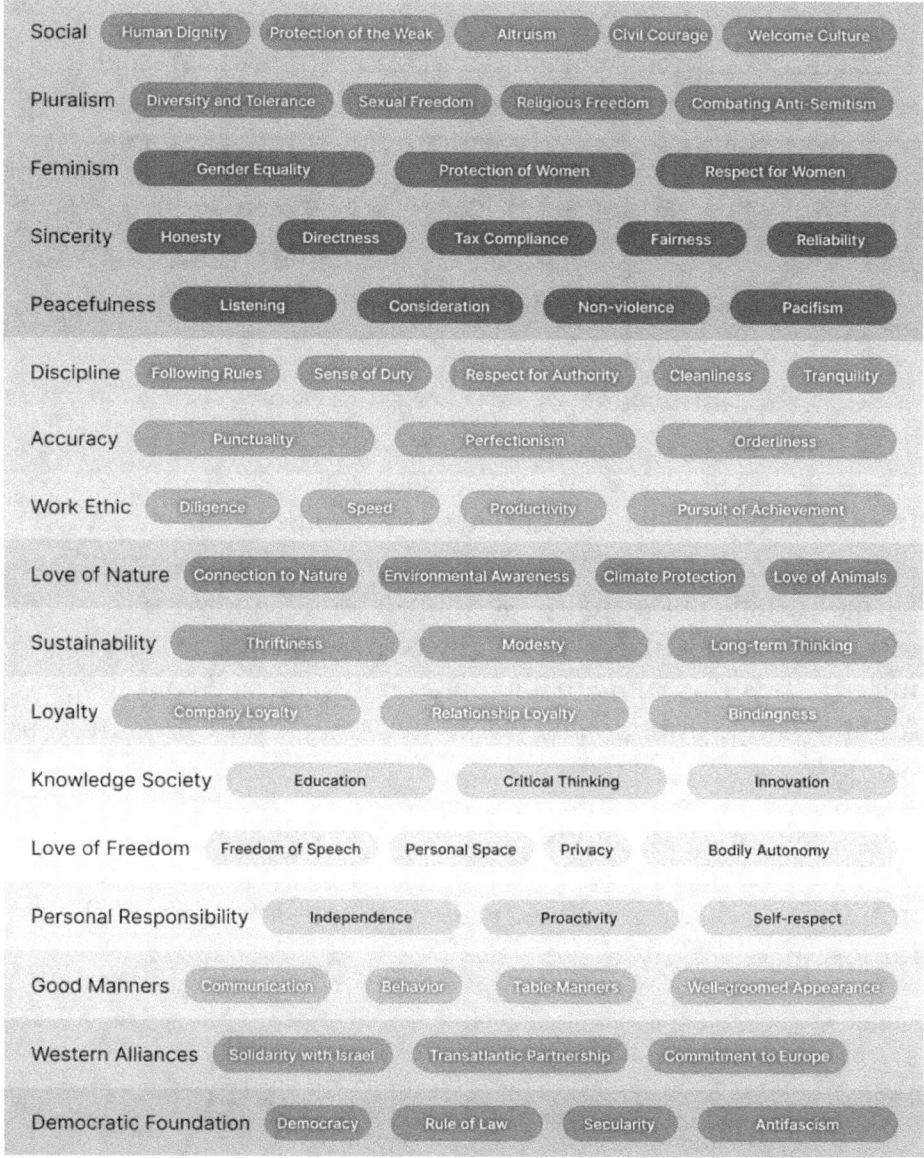

This system has the potential to lead us to a successful future.

The Weighting of Values

However, not all 64 values are of equal importance. For example, while non-violence as a cornerstone of a peaceful society is of enormous importance, the correct use of knives and forks plays a rather subordinate role for most people.

To capture this varying significance, we have introduced a scale of 1 to 4:

- 4 stands for "extremely important"
- 3 for "very important"
- 2 for "important"
- 1 for "less important"

In the evaluation, we consulted various sources: specialist literature, political positions, and - most valuable - interviews with Germans in Germany, Germans abroad, and with foreigners living in Germany. The central question was: "How important is this value to you personally on a scale of 1 to 4? And how important do you think this value is for Germany as a whole?"

The results were revealing: only on a few values was there a wide range of opinions, between "very important" and "less important." On most values, there was agreement about their importance.

24. THE GERMAN CULTURE CODE

In the following, we have highlighted the extremely important values in bold, while the less important ones are shown in a smaller font:

It's fascinating how differently values are weighted in German society! Some are so fundamental that they are part of German laws like unshakable pillars—think of respect for human dignity, diversity and tolerance, equality, the protection of women, the fight against anti-Semitism, non-violence, and freedom of expression. These values are the lifeblood of democracy, so important that they are set in stone.

But there are also values that shape German society without being enshrined in law books. They are like the glue that holds us together. There's the protection of the weak, the helping hand, moral courage—values that come from the heart. And of course, the typical German virtues: honesty, reliability, diligence, discipline and obedience, a sense of duty, and yes, even cleanliness!

We must not forget the political values that define Germany: democracy, the rule of law, secularism, and freedom of religion—they are the foundation for a successful and livable Germany.

And then there are the small, inconspicuous values that may not change the world but still enrich everyday lives.

With this colorful palette of values, we can create a cultural code that not only reflects the diversity of German society but also, like a compass, points the way we want to go together. It helps us preserve the treasures of German culture while forging new paths.

Should the Cultural Code Become Law?

We now have a compass for important success values—a cultural code for Germany. But do we have to turn this compass into an ironclad law right away? Do we really need even more rules and regulations to ensure a good coexistence?

Some seem to think so. The CDU, for example, which calls itself the "guiding culture party," demands in its basic program a "binding guiding culture without ifs and buts"—in other words, a guiding culture enforced with the hammer of the law.

But do we really want to live in a country where the state monitors us at every turn and punishes us for every little misstep? Wouldn't that stifle our freedom and turn the guiding culture into a rigid corset?

Between Law and Freedom: Where Rules Make Sense and Where They Restrict Us

Of course, we need rules to enable a peaceful coexistence. But it is important to understand where rules protect us and where they restrict us.

Laws are like the guardrails on the highway. They protect us from the serious accidents that can destroy our coexistence — violence, theft, fraud. Those who break through these guardrails must live with the consequences.

Cultural norms, on the other hand, are like the signposts in traffic. They help us find our way and treat each other with consideration. Punctuality, politeness, respect — they make life easier, but we don't want to enforce them with the whip of the law.

Imagine if we went to jail for being late, for infidelity, or for a little white lie! An absurd thought! Such things are not okay, but it is not the state's job to punish them. The social conscience of the community should decide here, not the jungle of paragraphs.

The Irony of Lawmakers: Rejecting Culture But Creating More and More Laws

It's paradoxical: The very politicians who act as champions of freedom and warn against a "restrictive" guiding culture are often the first to cry out for new laws for every problem. They preach tolerance but at the same time want to punish anyone who doesn't bow to the rainbow flag, criticizes NATO, or questions Israel.

Of course, these behaviors are not always okay. We have seen that diversity, tolerance, partnership with the West, and solidarity with Israel are important German values. But do we really have to swing the legal hammer for every misstep?

And even among those who advocate for a guiding culture, there are voices that, on the one hand, demand the reduction of bureaucracy, but on the other hand, want to cement the guiding culture with laws. So they want to reduce rules and regulation but then again create new rules and regulations. Where is the logic in that?

An example: The new naturalization law in Saxony-Anhalt. Since 2024, every migrant who wants to obtain German citizenship must explicitly recognize Israel's right to exist. In itself, supporting Israel is an important German value. But does it really have to be enforced by law? Wouldn't it make much more sense to convey this value through education and awareness-raising?

Cultural Code: More Freedom Through Fewer Laws

A cultural code is like a gentle guide that steers us in the right direction without restricting us with prohibitions and punishments. It appeals to our reason and motivates us to do the right thing on our own.

Our opinion: We need fewer laws and more value culture!

24. THE GERMAN CULTURE CODE

Illustration of making more laws

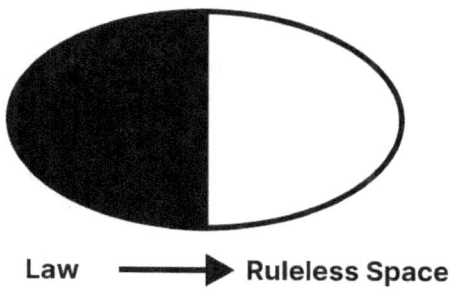

The black space represents laws, and the white space is the space without rules of conduct. Without culture, everything is either black or white. If you want more rules, you have to make more laws. If you want less guiding culture, it means either fewer rules of conduct (white space) or more laws (black space).

Illustration of having more culture

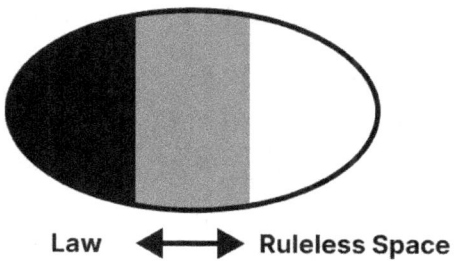

But an informal culture can set norms without restricting freedom through laws. This means we have fewer laws (less black) but also less unregulated space (less white). It fills the gap between the extremes and creates a space for a vibrant coexistence where values and norms guide us without restricting us.

The Art of Guidance: From a Wink to a Medal

It's about providing guidelines that help us find the right path. Culture can influence our behavior without banging the drum of the law.

There are many ways to motivate people to do the right thing without immediately threatening them with the hammer of the law. A warning look, a friendly word, the feeling of shame or pride, the recognition of the community – all these are subtle signals that steer us in the right direction.

And of course, the power of positive reinforcement! Those who stand up for others, who take responsibility, who achieve great things, are celebrated and honored. Such positive experiences inspire us and strengthen our desire to be a valuable member of society.

Cultural Code: A Compass for a Good Life Together

A cultural code is not a book full of paragraphs, but a compass that guides us through the jungle of life. It shows us which values are important to us and how we can treat each other with respect. It appeals to our reason and our heart, instead of bossing us around with punishments. It gives us the freedom to shape our own lives and at the same time encourages us to take responsibility for ourselves and our fellow human beings.

25. GUIDING CULTURE 2.0

Much has already been achieved: German guiding culture has been defined, and its three central elements - the guiding vision, the success story, and the cultural code - have been established. Of these elements, the cultural code is the centerpiece, as it contains the fundamental values on which German culture is based.

A Confusion of Terms - And Clarity About It

In the course of our discussion, we have wandered through a jungle of terms: culture, guiding culture, value culture, civilizational culture, success story, guiding vision... Admittedly, this diversity can make your head spin at first! But don't worry, we'll shed some light on the darkness! To understand the interplay of these terms, we need to take a close look at them.

What Does "Culture" Really Mean?

Right at the beginning of our journey, we established that culture has two faces: value culture and civilizational culture. Let's remember the diagram that illustrates this distinction:

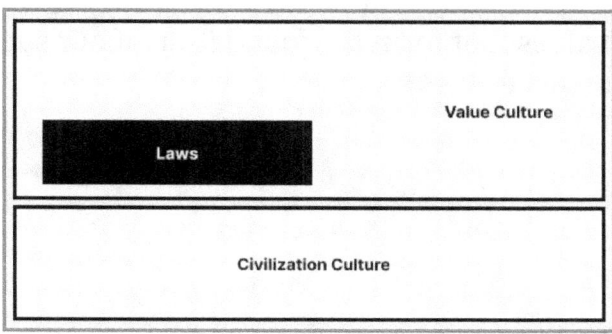

Civilizational culture encompasses areas such as art, food, literature, architecture, and clothing. While these aspects are important, they take a back seat in terms of the goal of ensuring Germany's long-term success. The guiding culture focuses exclusively on value culture.

Laws are also a component of value culture because they establish rules of conduct. All laws set standards for behavior in society, which makes them a part of value culture. But not every rule of conduct is enshrined in law. There are unwritten rules that are also part of value culture.

The Three Components of Guiding Culture

The guiding culture consists of three central elements: guiding visions, success stories, and guiding values.

- **Success stories:** These refer to the inspiring stories of our past. They show what has been successful in German history and thus offer orientation for the present.
- **Guiding visions:** These direct our gaze forward. They specify where our society should develop and how we can carry our values into the future.
- **The cultural code**: The center of the guiding culture. The cultural code is the most important element of the guiding culture. It expresses the crucial rules of conduct and values that form the foundation of our social coexistence.

This distinction is illustrated by another diagram:

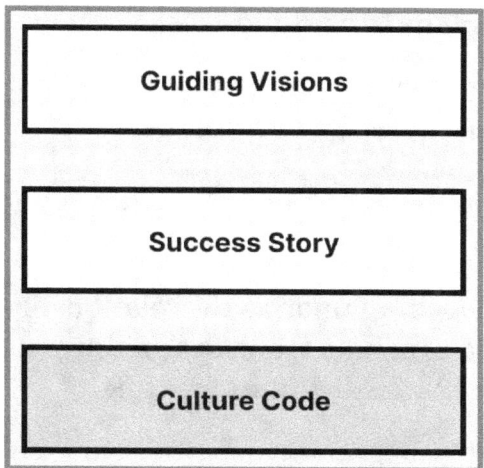

Code of Conduct

The code of conduct encompasses all rules of conduct, including the cultural code and laws. This relationship is also illustrated in a diagram:

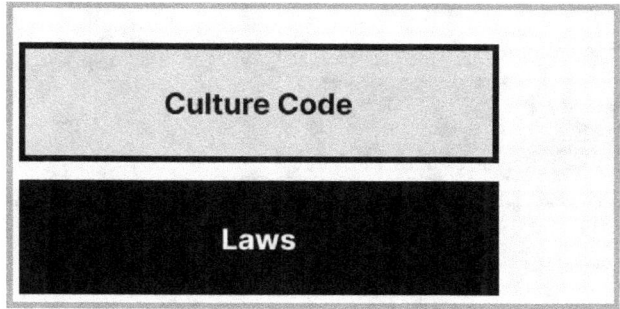

A code of conduct contains the particularly important values and norms that a society requires its members to follow.

Some values are so fundamental that they are not only part of the cultural code but are also enshrined in law. But laws and the cultural code go hand in hand, and the transition between the cultural code and the law is fluid.

As we have seen, laws alone are not sufficient as norms of behavior – we also need a cultural code.

The Relationship Between Culture, Code of Conduct, and Guiding Culture

The diagrams above summarize the relationship between culture, the code of conduct, and the guiding culture. We can now combine the three diagrams into one.

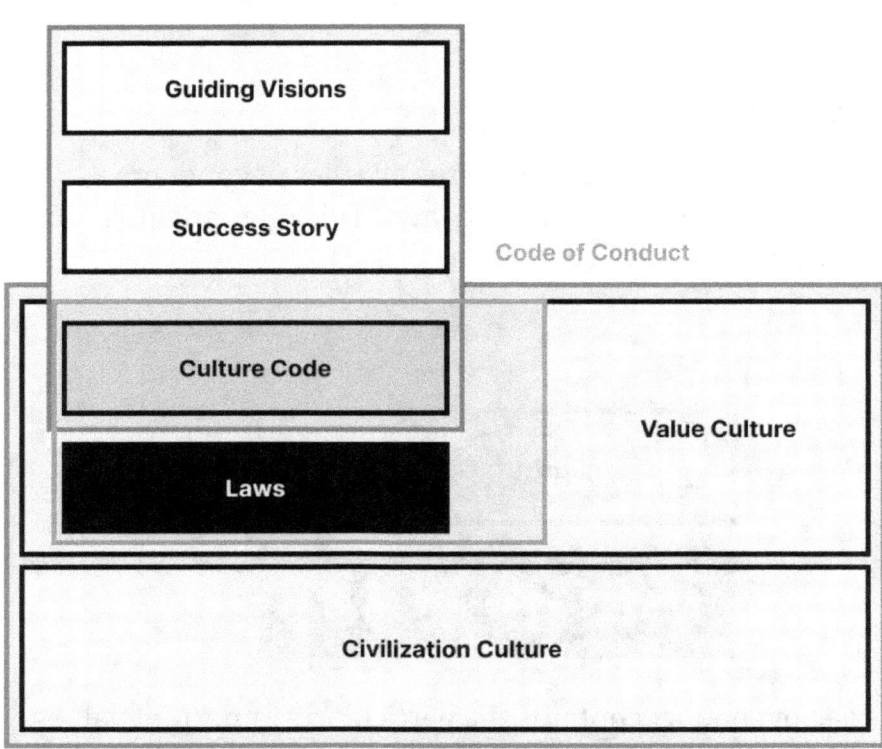

In this diagram, it is noticeable that while civilizational culture is an aspect of culture, it is not part of the guiding culture according to our definition. Furthermore, it shows that the central aspect present in culture, guiding culture, and the code of conduct is the cultural code. This cultural code is thus the centerpiece of everything. The guiding vision and the success story are of secondary importance.

The careful differentiation and definition of these terms show how closely they are linked. The guiding culture offers clear orientation on how the values of society can be cultivated and carried into the future. The cultural code remains the central core that determines social life and serves the long-term success of Germany.

26. ARGUMENTS AGAINST A GUIDING CULTURE

We have defined a guiding culture for Germany that should help Germany achieve its visions for the future. Just as companies have long known how important a strong corporate culture is for success, a society also needs shared values to thrive. Max Weber and modern economists have impressively demonstrated how crucial culture is to a country's success.

Nevertheless, the idea of a guiding culture remains controversial in Germany. Critics express many concerns: Is a guiding culture really necessary? Isn't it chauvinistic? Doesn't it hinder multiculturalism? Or does it even exclude people?

In this section, we want to take a closer look at the four main arguments against the guiding culture.

Argument 1: Do we need a guiding culture when we have laws?

"Germany doesn't need a guiding culture, but a constitutional state," says Christian Lindner of the FDP (freedom party of Germany). It is a frequently heard objection: for regulating behavior, creating order and ensuring security we have laws. Why do we need culture?

Of course, laws are important. They set the minimum requirements for our behavior to avoid punishment. But a functioning society needs more than just laws. It needs unwritten rules based on morals, decency, and mutual respect – what actually holds a society together.

26. ARGUMENTS AGAINST A GUIDING CULTURE

What laws cannot regulate

Let's look at a few examples that illustrate the importance of rules of conduct that go beyond laws.

Imagine a girl lying relaxed in the park in a bikini, sunbathing. Two young men sit down right next to her without asking and start looking at her with suggestive glances and making inappropriate comments. The girl feels constricted, uncomfortable, and threatened. Although the men do not make physical contact and formally break no law, their behavior is disrespectful and intrusive.

Or imagine a woman riding alone in an elevator. A man gets in and stands uncomfortably close to her, looks her straight in the eye, and looks her up and down. The woman feels uncomfortable and exposed. The man may not have broken any law, but his behavior leaves the woman anxious and insecure.

Another example: A group of young people are boisterous in a restaurant, smacking their lips loudly, and disturbing the other guests. They laugh loudly, shout at each other, and turn up their music so loud that the other guests can hardly talk to each other anymore. The romantic dinner of a couple at the next table is disturbed, the atmosphere in the restaurant is poisoned. Although the young people have not broken any law, their behavior is inconsiderate and selfish.

These examples illustrate that laws alone are not enough to guarantee a harmonious coexistence. A guiding culture that goes beyond mere obedience to the law is necessary to provide orientation in the gray areas of human behavior.

Argument 2: Isn't guiding culture simply chauvinistic?

The German term "Leitkultur" ("guiding culture") triggers negative associations for many people. It is often associated with national arrogance and the notion that one's own culture is superior to others. But this interpretation falls short.

The word "Leiten" can be translated into English as "guiding" or "leading." So it is true that "Leitkultur" could be understood in the sense of "leading culture" - a culture that is supposed to be the best and dominate others. But that is not the meaning we use here. For us, "Leitkultur" means a "guiding culture, one that helps others. It is about creating a common basis that helps all people in Germany - regardless of their origin - to integrate and be part of society.

Furthermore, the guiding culture is not an exclusive club where only Germans set the tone and tell migrants how to live. It is an offer to everyone to agree on common values and behaviors that include respect, tolerance, and consideration. This guiding culture applies not only to migrants but also to Germans.

Argument 3: Doesn't guiding culture hinder multiculturalism?

Critics of the guiding culture fear that it forces people to fully adapt to a German way of life - whether it's eating German food, drinking German beer, reading Goethe, or celebrating Christmas and Easter in the traditional way. These fears are reinforced when politicians equate guiding culture with customs, traditions, literature, and food.

If one really were to base a guiding culture on such a civilizational culture, the image of a German culture and its behavioral rules could look like this:

- **Customs**: Visit the Oktoberfest and celebrate carnival.

26. ARGUMENTS AGAINST A GUIDING CULTURE

- **Food**: Eat bratwurst, Black Forest cake, and apple strudel.
- **Literature**: Read Goethe and Schiller.
- **Holidays**: Celebrate Christmas with a decorated tree.

Such a cultural code of civilizational culture would indeed be exclusionary. It would force people to adopt certain traditions in order to be considered "belonging to Germany" or "True German".

But such a definition of guiding culture at the level of civilizational culture has nothing to do with the guiding culture as we understand it in this book. The German guiding culture is based on shared values and behaviors that shape the social coexistence, i.e. a value culture.

A practical example: In Germany, there are many Muslims who have internalized the values of German value culture - they are punctual, respectful, hard-working, environmentally conscious, helpful, and disciplined - and yet they lead lives that differ from the traditional "German" lifestyle. They do not eat pork, celebrate Ramadan but not Christmas, and pray several times a day. Their behavior is 100% part of the German guiding culture!

On the other hand, there are people who cultivate the typical "German" lifestyle - they celebrate Christmas, drink German beer, go to the Oktoberfest, but their behavior often contradicts the basic values of German society. They are unpunctual, disrespectful, lazy, or inconsiderate of their fellow human beings. Their behavior is not part of the German guiding culture.

This leads us to an important realization: multiculturalism and a strong guiding culture ("Leitkultur") can go hand in hand. This is illustrated in the following diagram:

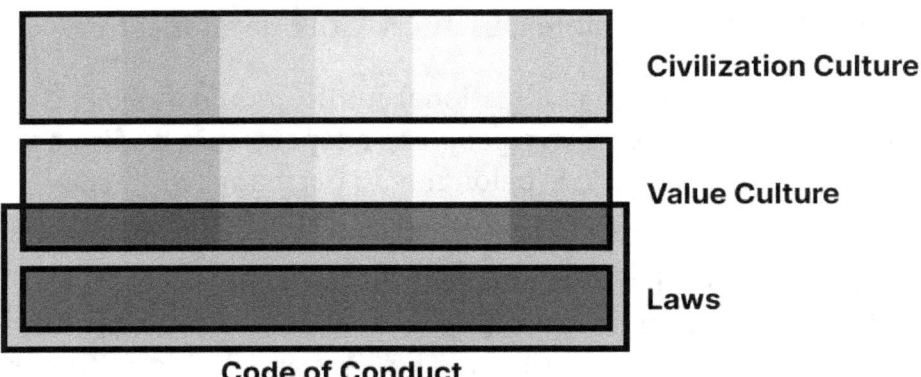

We have illustrated different cultures with different colors. As we can see, laws are shown in a neutral color to demonstrate that they apply to everyone, regardless of culture.

In addition, there are also rules of conduct. However, these do not affect civilizational culture - your favorite music, your food, your clothing, all of that is up to you! It's about the values and behaviors that form the glue of German society. Here, too, a wide range of opinions and forms of expression is allowed. There are only a few points on which all Germans, as a society, agree - the German consensus on values - and that is the guiding culture.

Thus, multiculturalism is possible even with a strong guiding culture. A strong guiding culture based on shared values and behaviors allows us to celebrate diversity while maintaining strong cohesion. It is like a colorful garden where a wide variety of flowers bloom side by side, yet form a harmonious whole.

26. ARGUMENTS AGAINST A GUIDING CULTURE

Argument 4: Does a Guiding Culture Restrict People Too Much?

"A guiding culture restricts personal freedom!" - this objection often haunts the debate. Critics fear that it forces us into a rigid corset and leaves no room for individuality.

This criticism is often based on the misunderstanding that a guiding culture functions like a strict legal code enforced with punishments. It is true that there are political forces that demand such bindingness. The CDU (Conservative party of Germany), for example, proclaims in its basic program a "binding guiding culture without ifs and buts." But that does not correspond to our idea of a guiding culture.

Our guiding culture is not a law book, but a compass that gives us orientation and helps us treat each other with respect. If someone does not adhere to it, there is no prison sentence - rather, society reacts with critical glances or comments. However, those who adhere to the guiding culture receive recognition and respect.

In this way, a guiding culture promotes a harmonious coexistence without restricting personal freedom. It is like a friendly signpost that helps us find the right path without forcing us.

All the arguments against a guiding culture mentioned above have a valid basis but are not directed against the kind of guiding culture that we propose. Our guiding culture is not an instrument of oppression, but a tool for understanding that helps us grow together in a diverse society.

27. NEED FOR A GUIDING CULTURE

We have seen that a strong guiding culture is crucial to Germany's success and that all the arguments raised against a guiding culture fall flat. It is therefore obvious that we need to consciously work on the German guiding culture to ensure that it remains a "success culture" and continues to guarantee maximum success in the future.

We need to stop a further decline of German culture and must rekindle the embers of old German values that have crumbled to ashes in recent decades and thus save German success.

From Shining Example to a Shadow of Its Former Self

Just 20 years ago, Germany was a shining example to the world, a beacon of success. It was a global leader in exports, innovation, business, and even sports. When I traveled the world at the beginning of the millennium, I felt respect and admiration when I said, "I come from Germany."

But this image is cracking! Germany is at a crossroads: either it succeeds in reinventing itself and reviving its culture of success, or the country will continue to lose influence and sink into the shadow of its former self.

From Export Miracle to Decline

In the 1980s, Germany was the export world champion. It was still able to maintain this position at the beginning of the 2000s. But in 2023, the world looks different: Germany has fallen back to third place, overtaken by China and the USA. China now exports more than twice as much as Germany!

27. NEED FOR A GUIDING CULTURE

Innovative Power at a Crossroads

Germany was once the land of great inventors, the cradle of groundbreaking ideas. Patents were the nation's pride, emblematic of a relentless innovative spirit. But today, the engine that once powered global advancements has slowed considerably. The number of patents filed each year has lagged far behind those of the USA, China, and Japan—countries that each filed more than double the number of patents as Germany in 2023.

A striking example is the Transrapid, a cutting-edge technology capable of moving people at speeds of 600 km/h with silent magnetic propulsion. Developed in Germany and tested on the first Transrapid line in Emsland, north-west Germany, as early as 1980, it was a remarkable innovation. Yet, despite its potential, the technology was never put into use within Germany. Instead, it found a home in China, where thousands of kilometers of Transrapid lines now connect major cities. This missed opportunity is a bittersweet reminder of what Germany once pioneered but ultimately left behind.

The former innovative strength is also eroding in new key areas such as genetic engineering, artificial intelligence, and renewable energies. While the world is progressing inexorably, Germany is in danger of losing touch and becoming a spectator.

Economic Splendor Fades

The decline becomes even more frightening when you look at the country's prosperity. In 1982, Germany was the epitome of wealth and stability. Per capita income was then 34,000 USD - among the top of the world and well ahead of Singapore. But things have changed dramatically. While Singapore has caught up and eventually overtaken in impressive fashion in recent decades, Germany has stagnated. In 2022, per capita income in Singapore was 85,000 USD, while Germany recorded only 49,000 USD. Prosperity is growing elsewhere, and Germany is lagging behind its former peers.

Even Sport Reflects the Decline

As if Germany's decline in business and innovation were not worrying enough, this trend is even evident in sport. In 1992, Germany dominated the Olympic Games, winning 33 gold medals - an impressive 13% of all gold medals awarded and was competing for first place overall with Russia and the USA. But in 2024, it only achieved 12 gold medals, just 3.6% and a meager 10th place overall. Here, too, the symbol of German strength and discipline is fading, and the country has to watch other nations overtake it.

What Led to This Decline?

There are many attempted explanations - from the debt crisis to the ECB's interest rate policy, the refugee crisis, unfair competition from China, to the Ukraine war. But is that the whole truth? Germany survived two world wars, with more than 50 million deaths. It has experienced hyperinflation of over 25,000% and yet has always regained its former strength. So what is the real reason?

The Transformation of German Success Culture

The answer lies deeper. It is a transformation of German success culture. Culture is not static - it is constantly changing. But in the last 50 years, this change has reached an

27. NEED FOR A GUIDING CULTURE

unprecedented speed and intensity. The post-war period, the student movement of the 1960s, reunification, globalization, the digital revolution, and the migration crisis - all these events have left deep marks on German value culture.

Traditional values such as punctuality, thrift, discipline, attention to detail and respect for rules have lost importance, while individualism, pluralism, and self-realization are increasingly coming to the fore. Even in the world of work, the focus has shifted - flexibility and work-life balance are the dominant themes today, while hard-work and diligence are less important.

These shifts prompt important questions about Germany's direction: Is the nation losing the values that once underpinned its strength? Has the relentless drive for success been tempered, or even overshadowed, by a growing preference for comfort and leisure? Reflecting on these questions could shed light on why Germany no longer holds the leading position it once commanded.

Awareness for the Future

The prosperity Germany enjoys today is the result of hard-won achievements from the 18th, 19th, and 20th centuries. The Germans of those times fostered a success-driven culture that created prosperity not only for themselves but contributed globally. Observing from the outside, it's striking to consider that with today's mindset, the immense challenges of the last 300 years might have been far more difficult to overcome.

For Germany to continue building on the strengths of its past and aim for new heights, it may be time to strengthen its cultural foundation and renew its values. Revitalizing the spirit of success could help Germany reclaim its place among the world's leaders.

28. PRESERVATION OF THE GERMAN SUCCESS CULTURE

We've already achieved a lot in the previous chapters: We've defined a guiding culture with a clear vision and a success story. We delved deep into German culture and explored its 17 basic principles with 64 values and hundreds of rules of conduct. It became clear that this culture has contributed significantly to Germany's success. But now we are at a turning point: German culture has been changing, and Germany has lost its leading role in many areas.

Imagine we are standing on a mountaintop, looking back at the path we have climbed. We see the successes we have celebrated, but also the challenges that have pushed us to our limits. But the journey is not over yet! Ahead of us lies a new summit, even higher, even more demanding. Are we ready for the ascent?

Values in Danger

Which values are the keys to this success? Which ones must we cherish like a treasure, and which ones are in danger of sinking into the sands of time?

Values such as equality, tolerance, diversity, sexual fredom, climate protection, and a welcome culture are loudly proclaimed in the streets – they have become an integral part of Germany's guiding culture over the last 30 years. But other, equally important values are in danger of fading like an old photograph. These are the values that affectdemocracy, such as freedom of expression and the rule of law, but also the typical German virtues: punctuality, discipline, a sense of duty, and diligence. These cornerstones of German society are crumbling, and we must strengthen them before they collapse.

What are the best ways to avoid the decline in values? We will delve deeper into this question in the next chapters.

Patriotism: An Often Neglected Value

A sleeping giant that we must awaken is patriotism. In Germany, there is often a lack of courage to be proud of one's own achievements. The shadows of the past make Germans hesitate to celebrate their national identity. But this pride is the lifeblood of any culture and a source of strength. Patriotism does not mean nationalism, but the honest recognition of Germany's achievements - be it in science, technology, culture, or social cohesion. It is the flame that warms and unites us.

But how can we revive this patriotism in a time when national identity is often viewed critically? We will delve deeper into this question in the next chapters.

Cultural Differences Within Germany

Germany is not a monolithic entity, but a multifaceted mosaic. East and West, migrants and natives, elites in media, politics, and finance, and "ordinary" citizens - each group has its own perspective and its own values. To shape the future of German culture, we need to understand this mosaic and recognize how each group contributes its own touch of color to German value culture.

But how can we reconcile these different perspectives and create a common foundation of values? This question, too, will be answered in the next chapters.

28. PRESERVATION OF THE GERMAN SUCCESS CULTURE

Political Differences

Politics also mixes the colors on the palette. Conservatives (CDU, CSU, AfD) value diligence, personal responsibility, a sense of duty, and thrift, while progressives (SPD, Greens, Die Linke) emphasize tolerance, climate protection, a welcoming culture, and equality.

In principle, German society has developed away from conservative values towards progressive values in recent decades. This development has created more openness and inclusivity, but it has also slowed economic growth.

We will see that conservative and progressive values do not have to be mutually exclusive – that we can revive conservative values without sacrificing progressive values.

But how do we achieve this balance? How can we unite conservative and progressive values to create a strong and sustainable Germany? In the next chapters, we will examine this question in detail.

Dangers to the Value Culture

However, the change in values is not just a shift between conservative and progressive principles. It is more complex, more multifaceted. Where does this change come from? Who are the actors changing German culture? Are these changes positive, negative, or perhaps both?

There are dangers to German value culture from various sides: elites who, detached from reality, pursue their own ideas of culture; globalization, which softens national identity; migrants who bring their own culture, and educational institutions that promote ideological currents that dilute German values.

In the next chapters, we will take a close look at these sources of danger and develop strategies to protect German culture.

The Role of Migration

Immigration is an enrichment, but also a challenge. Many migrants struggle with German values. But is that really due to their cultural roots? Or due to a lack of cultural roots?

They often come to Germany as adolescents without being firmly rooted in their native culture or German culture. Migrants who come to a new country without family support often float in a cultural vacuum – a dangerous state that can lead to disorientation and behaviors outside the cultural norm.

This vacuum is a far greater danger than the fact that migrants live their own native culture. Because, as we will see, many elements of German and their native cultures agree.

But how can we better integrate migrants into German society and help them find their way in German culture? This question will also be addressed in the next chapters.

The Influence of Islam

Many of the migrants have a Muslim background, and the proportion of the Muslim population in Germany will continue to grow. This is perceived by some as a threat to German culture.

But Islam is not the enemy of German values. On the contrary: many Islamic values coincide with traditional German values.

28. PRESERVATION OF THE GERMAN SUCCESS CULTURE

Islam can even help to strengthen conservative values such as a sense of duty and discipline. Especially in a time when these values are losing importance, the influence of Islamic values can help to bring them back to the forefront.

In the next chapters, we will examine the role of Islam in German society in more detail and investigate how we can use the positive aspects of this religion to strengthen the traditional German guiding culture.

How We Can Preserve German Guiding Culture

The most important question remains: How can we preserve and strengthen the German guiding culture? Education is key! We must promote a strong values base in German schools. Values such as openness, tolerance, and climate protection are already being taught, but what about diligence, discipline, thrift, and punctuality? These values, which are so important for Germany's success, must be brought back into focus.

In addition to education in schools, there are many other approaches that we will present in the next chapters to protect and promote the German success culture.

Extension of this Book: The Preservation of the German Success Culture

All of these topics are of crucial importance, and we have already touched on many of these points. But this first step was just the beginning! To really do justice to these questions and challenges, we need a deeper analysis.

In the sequel, which will be published under the title "The Preservation of the German Success Culture," we will intensively address these complex topics.

"The Preservation of the German Success Culture" is still in progress. If you have any ideas or opinions on the topics raised that should be discussed further, please do not hesitate to contact me. Maybe you will even become a co-author!

What do you think about this book?

I would be delighted if you would take a moment to write your opinion about the book on Amazon. Your opinion not only helps other readers discover the book but also supports me as an author. Every review - whether short or long - makes a big difference.

Thank you very much for your support!

www.ingramcontent.com/pod-product-compliance
Lightning Source LLC
Chambersburg PA
CBHW071018240526
45469CB00006BD/1978